WHAT PEOPLE ARE SAYING ABOUT
JESUS FIRST, JESUS ALWAYS

"Jeffrey Smith is an incredible communicator of the gospel with a heart for all people. *Jesus First, Jesus Always* is not just the title of His book, it is the anthem of his life! I know this book will inspire you to live out your God given purpose."

- Rich Wilkerson Jr. | Lead Pastor, Vous Church and Author, *Sandcastle Kings*

"In *Jesus First, Jesus Always*, Dr. Jeffrey Smith will help you to see your life through the right lens. He'll give you Jesus spectacles so that you can see clearly who Jesus is and who He created you to be. Don't miss out on the chance to look past what you can see with the naked eye, check this book out!"

- Levi Lusko | Author, *Swipe Right*

"You can sense such a great sense of joy for what is being said as you read through the pages of *Jesus First, Jesus Always*. Joy to make Biblical truths easy to understand. Joy that points to knowing Jesus more and becoming more like Him. It's a contagious joy that I know will bring great strength to those who read it."

- Marcus Mecum | Senior Pastor, 7 Hills Church

"Jesus has radically changed my life and I know He can change yours too. The message Jeff shares in *Jesus First, Jesus Always* is one of radical hope that I know will inspire you to fix your eyes on Jesus as you run towards the purpose God has for your life."

- Christine Caine | Founder, A21 and Propel Women and Author, *Unashamed*

"I love Pastor Jeffrey Smith. His infectious disposition, love for Jesus and desire to serve the local church and see people come to a saving knowledge of Christ is so evident in *Jesus First, Jesus Always*. It will undoubtedly impact you to do and feel the same."

- Brian Houston | Founder and Global Senior Pastor, Hillsong Church

"I feel like this beautiful and broken world we live in is continually becoming more and more about self-interest, often to the detriment of everyone and everything else. As Jeffrey so well asks us, are we living "me first, me always?" I believe this book will help many understand the need as well as the great benefits of a life that declares, *Jesus First, Jesus Always*."

- Ben Houston | Lead Pastor, Hillsong California

"Jeffrey Smith wears many hats. I've had the privilege to know him as friend. His life models *Jesus First, Jesus Always*. This book is as brilliant as it is authentic. If you desire to live the life that God intended for you to live, then this book is for you."

- Chris Durso | Pastor, Misfit NYC and Author, *The Heist* and *Misfit*

"Jeffrey Smith is a trusted voice . . . a man of integrity, creativity and passion for people. I love this book and the heart behind it. If life isn't about Jesus, what's it about. A lot of leaders can get caught up in the fads and trends of church . . . but what I love and appreciate about Jeffrey is that he is drawing a line in the sand with *Jesus First, Jesus Always*. I believe this book will bring you great comfort and clarity and will realign your life back to the main thing, JESUS."

- Chad Veach | Lead Pastor, Zoe Church L.A. and Author, Unreasonable Hope

"When I think of the statement *Jesus First, Jesus Always*, I have to think of the life of my friends Jeffrey and Amy Smith. This book is simply the overflow of lives well lived. A couple who radically loves Jesus and inspires all of us to do the same. Read this book and come back to your first love, the lover of your soul, Jesus."

- Jabin Chavez | Senior Pastor, City Light Church L.V.

"Jeffrey Smith is a brilliant thought leader and a great friend. His book, *Jesus First, Jesus Always*, brings us fresh ideas about how our faith in Jesus can shape how we live. Jeffrey brings to life the joy of knowing Jesus as a person, not just a philosophy. This book will bring clarity and inspiration for living out your journey of faith."

- Kent Munsey | Lead Pastor,
City Church Chicago

JESUS FIRST
JESUS ALWAYS

JESUS FIRST
JESUS ALWAYS

the life you were **meant** to live

JEFFREY SMITH

23 22 21 20 19 18   8 7 6 5 4 3 2 1

Published by:
Emerge Publishing, llc
9521B Riverside Parkway, Suite 243
Tulsa, Oklahoma 74137
Phone: 888.407.4447
www.EmergePublishing.com

Published in association with The Fedd Agency, Inc., a literary agency.

Library of Congress Cataloging-in-Publication Data

ISBN: 978-1-943127-94-8 Hardcover
ISBN: 978-1-943127-95-5 Digital/E-book

BISAC Category:
REL012120   RELIGION/Christian Life/Spiritual Growth
REL067040   RELIGION/Christian Theology/Christology
REL006710   RELIGION/Biblical Studies/Jesus, the Gospels & Acts

Printed in the United States of America.

for my family.
_____

CONTENTS

FOREWORD

I love leaders. I love leadership. I believe we are all called, to lead people in a direction that makes a difference far beyond our lifetime. Yet I also believe, the best way to actually lead is to be a follower of Jesus. He has already carved the path, in blood red, that leads to life and hope and peace and true fulfillment. And this is why I love Jeffrey Smith. He's a dear friend, he is a songwriter, he is a phenomenal dad, a loving pastor and husband, and a creative genius. But I think what I love about Jeff the most is that he follows Jesus so well. I don't think there is a higher compliment I could give any person that I love. He doesn't want to make people "like him." He wants to show people who Jesus is! Because when we know Him, walk with Him and love like He did things change. In fact, perhaps Jesus first, Jesus always is the goal. Maybe people won't even remember us! Because we reflected Jesus so well. It reminds me of when I first met Jeff. Or more aptly, heard him sing. I was in a church meeting in Hawaii, I had my eyes closed during the singing and I heard a voice that was just amazing. I kept thinking, "Wow, this guy can sing!" I overheard somebody next to me, say "Man, this brother can SING." When I opened my eyes, to my shock, there was this white guy with glasses and a crew cut! I couldn't believe it. Had I not actually seen him, I would have thought he was somebody else. At the end of the day, maybe that's the point of our entire lives! People are impacted by Jesus through us first! They are impacted by him long after we go. People see a love, a kindness and joy, in us that doesn't actually make sense, when you see "us" for who we really are! Which might even lead to the greatest question of all time. Who exactly is Jesus? This book is one that is going to help me on this journey. Not the leadership journey, but the "followership" journey. Doesn't sound as cool, but what it produces goes a lot deeper than "cool" ever could. It will change your life! I'm gonna follow Jesus first. I want to follow Jesus always. I pray this book gets in the hands of many, and I'm glad it found its way to you.

- Carl Lentz

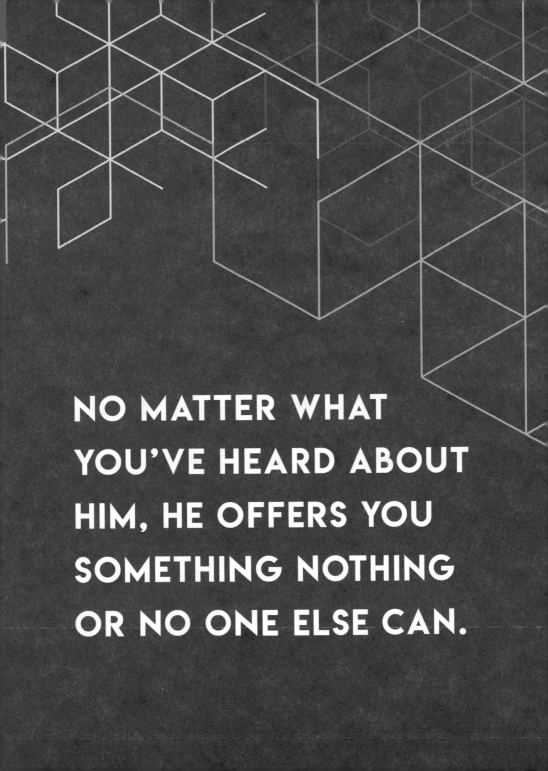

NO MATTER WHAT
YOU'VE HEARD ABOUT
HIM, HE OFFERS YOU
SOMETHING NOTHING
OR NO ONE ELSE CAN.

INTRODUCTION

I didn't know I needed glasses until I was seventeen years old. It was 1989.

When my mom got me out of school early to see the eye doctor, I was mostly thinking about how I would look with glasses. Maybe I could get some Ralph Lauren frames with the little Polo guy on the side—that wouldn't be so bad. As I tried them on for the first time, I was asking myself if I could really pull off the studious look. I wasn't thrilled about it, nor was I convinced this whole ordeal was even necessary. I put the glasses back in their case and didn't wear them out of the store.

On the drive home, my mom suggested I go ahead and put them on. When I did, something unexpected happened. I forgot about the brand. I forgot about my appearance. I was looking at the trees passing by at fifty-five miles per hour and seeing the details for the first time. I shouted, "Those trees have leaves! I can see blades of grass! Mom, I can *read* everything!" I remember seeing the crisp edges of the letters of street signs. I discovered that streetlights do not have a ten-foot glow around them at night as I had always thought. No more squinting at the movies. I was finally seeing the world the way I was meant to see it. I loved those glasses.

I'm not a philosophical optometrist, but I am inviting you to join me on a journey of discovery. I believe we are meant to live a certain kind of life. I believe there is a way of viewing the world that takes everything you've ever known and brings a clarity that was previously unimaginable.

You may have never realized there is a different way of seeing this world. You may think you get along just fine. Or maybe you fully recognize that things are cloudy and unfocused. You have been searching for this clarity in your life. Please come along as we find focus in who Jesus really is. No matter what you have heard about him, he offers you something nothing, or no one, else can.

Jesus once referred to himself as the light of the world. That's a beautiful name. It's also a rather huge statement. In ancient Greece, people believed that visual perception was achieved by light beams that emanated from our eyes, illuminating whatever we looked at. It was not some fringe theory; it was the prevailing premise among the great thinkers of the world, including Plato and Ptolemy. People generally believed this premise for nearly a thousand years until it was discovered that we don't see because of light coming *from* our eyes, we see because of the light that is refracted from objects, which goes *into* our eyes. The *Intromission Theory* is commonly recognized today.

Human beings do not have the ability to emanate light. As a Superman fan, this is disappointing. The good news, though, is that light makes things visible. Everyone knows that now. It still seems that there is an ongoing philosophical debate on how *truth* is discovered, though. Many believe truth comes from within, and whatever they perceive is a reflection of what emanates from their own eyes. When Jesus said he was the light of the world, he was inviting us to see the way the world looks when his light is reflected into our lives. His is a light that was first. It was here before we were. It is a light that always is; it is eternal. His is a light that will become everything in between, the through line of our lives.

I am a pastor, so I'll be referring to the Bible quite a

bit in this book. Many people do not believe the Bible is a book that is inspired by God. Many do not believe a book so old could say anything relevant in modern times. I am not one of those people. I believe the Bible is a book given to us from a loving God who wants to be known. I believe it contains a message of hope, purpose, redemption, and ultimately, love. I don't believe this because I am a Christian; I am a Christian because I believe this.

As I am writing, I am the oldest I have ever been, and unfortunately, my vision is not improving. It's actually getting worse. Like everything else in this life, it's gradually fading away. When I get a new prescription every few years, I have a similar experience to the first time I put on those glasses so many years ago. I'm shocked by how beautiful the world looks when I view it with such clarity.

In the same way, my whole life is continually being refocused because of Jesus. Every day I continue to learn about him, so every day is an opportunity to see life in a dynamic new way.

I recently watched (through man tears) a video of blind children in India seeing for the first time, thanks to an amazing surgery. I will never forget their wonder and joy the moment they first saw their parents. Knowing Jesus is like that, but even better. It's like getting a new pair of glasses. Seeing for the first time. It's like coming back to life when you were dead before. I pray this book will be that for you. I hope it will help you see the world anew, as clearly as I did in Lens Crafters back in 1989.

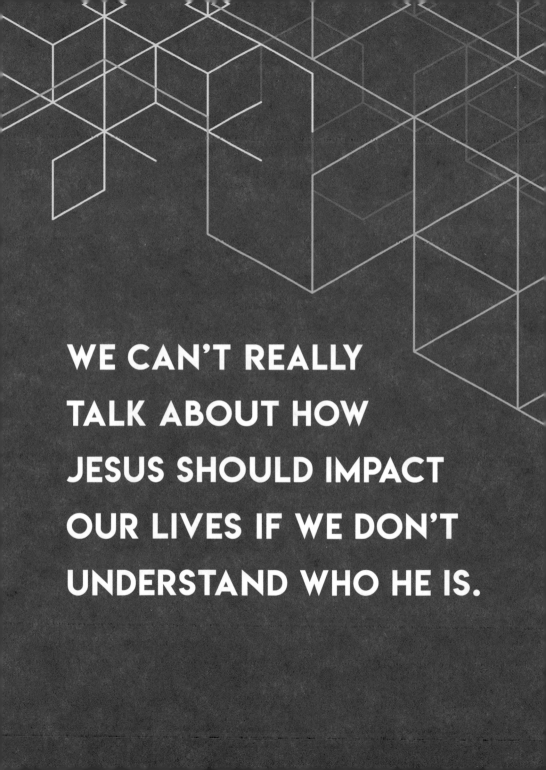

WE CAN'T REALLY TALK ABOUT HOW JESUS SHOULD IMPACT OUR LIVES IF WE DON'T UNDERSTAND WHO HE IS.

CHAPTER ONE:
who am i?

"'You are a king, then!' said Pilate. Jesus answered, 'You say that I am a king. In fact, the reason I was born and came into the world is to testify to the truth. Everyone on the side of truth listens to me.'"

— John 18:37

MILLION DOLLAR QUESTION

"Who is Keyser Söze?" That was the question posed in an ad campaign for one of my favorite films growing up, *The Usual Suspects*.

Keyser Söze is a nearly mythical character—the boogeyman of the criminal world. Most criminals and authorities don't even believe he exists. Though it seems nobody has ever seen him, five con men in the movie are blackmailed and threatened into working for him. After an epic gun battle replete with explosions and Caesar-esque betrayals, the mystery of Söze's identity is unraveled in the testimony of one of the remaining survivors, Verbal Kint, who describes him this way: "Keaton always said, 'I don't believe in God, but I'm afraid of him.' Well, I believe in God, and the only thing that scares me is Keyser Söze."

Without divulging too much of the ingenious plot twist, let me just say, the question permeates the whole film until the lead agent pieces together the evidence that finally reveals Söze's identity, but it's too late.

Knowing Keyser Söze's true identity alters the way we think about the movie and how we interact with the characters. If the suspects had known more about him, they probably could have avoided the majority of the trouble they found themselves in. If the detectives had real evidence of his existence, they probably would have treated the suspects differently in order to catch Söze. Knowing he exists and who he really is would have been a game changer for the authorities, the suspects, and of course, the audience.

Watching the movie a second time is a completely different experience. So many details taunt you, screaming, "You missed me! You missed me!"

I now know who Keyser Söze is; therefore, I understand the film. You don't have to see the film to understand the concept, though. Knowing Darth Vader is Luke's father changes the way you think about Star Wars.

In the same way, knowing who Jesus really is changes the game completely. We can't really talk about how Jesus should impact our lives if we don't understand who he is. The fact that he lived and walked the earth is not generally debated; there is more than adequate historical proof for that. Even atheist and agnostic scholars typically concede that the historical Jesus existed.

But who *was* he?

I believe we can know the answer to that question. As a matter of fact, I believe we are *meant* to know the answer. Whether you are a skeptic or a person of faith, I invite you to search with me.

Who was Jesus? A great teacher? Wise sage? Legendary rabbi? Wizard? Magician? Best beard ever?

Who was Jesus?

YOU CAN TELL A LOT ABOUT SOMEONE BY WHAT THEY LOVE.

WHO AM I?

You can tell a lot about someone by what they love. If you want to get a good glimpse into who a person truly is, ask the ones they spend the most time with. I decided to try an experiment. I asked my wife and three kids separately to quickly name something I love. Apparently, in a nearly unanimous vote, I love football more than anything in the universe, although my youngest daughter, Zoe, informed me that my greatest love is "tickling her a lot." Not a single, "Obviously, Jesus" or "Dad, you love us."

I love my wife, Amy. I love my kiddos, Mia, Jude, and Zoe. I love soul music, thrillers and horror films, mango-shrimp sushi rolls, red velvet cake (don't judge), being a part of my church family, producing music, and directing films.

If I'm honest, most of the things I love have to do with how they make me feel. That's hard to admit. I find tremendous meaning and purpose in giving my time to others and serving people, but I'm probably not as altruistic as I'd like to be. I'm growing. I'm learning. I'm becoming. I'm a work in progress.

Human love is typically predicated on conditions or some type of gratification. Knowing this helps me understand the difference between my conditional love and the unconditional love Jesus demonstrates. Jesus' unconditional love is never about what someone does or who someone is; it is about what *he* does and who *he* is. More on this to come . . .

WHAT DID HIS FOLLOWERS SAY ABOUT HIM?

Jesus happened to have twelve men who followed him everywhere for about three years, and even they were uncertain about who he was. "Who is this man?" was a pretty common question among the disciples.

In the gospel of Mark, the author portrays Jesus' disciples as bumbling fools (which gives us all a little hope, doesn't it?). They're thick-skulled. They never really get it right. They're always confused when he teaches, let alone when he performs miracles.

Jesus slept as the wind and the waves tossed their boat around in the middle of the Sea of Galilee, and his disciples accused him of not caring that they were all going to die. As Jesus rubbed the sleep from his eyes, face palming once again at the disciples' lack of understanding, he stood up, called out to the waves, and they stopped.

"Who is this? Even the wind and the waves obey him!" (Mark 4:41).

When they landed on shore, things got weirder. Sitting on the beach was a man possessed by demons. He had lived away from society for years, sleeping among the tombs, naked, and tormented. It was clear people had tried to subdue him because he was in chains, but the chains had been broken because he had, like, Hulk powers, *for real*. He was loud, violent, and completely controlled by his demons.

As Jesus stepped out of the boat, the man fell to his knees, yelling, "What do you want with me, Jesus, Son of the Most High God?" The demons knew who Jesus was better than the disciples did. That had to freak the disciples out!

Jesus drove out the demons and then, right after that, the disciples got confused again when Jesus healed a woman and raised a little girl from the dead. They just didn't get it. They knew he could heal the sick, drive out demons, forgive the sinners, and calm the waves, but they just couldn't put their finger on who this guy was.

Not long after that, Jesus healed a blind man by spitting in his face while they were on the road to a nearby town and then asked his disciples a very pointed question: "Who do people say I am?" Nice road trip conversation, Jesus.

Looking around at each other, probably trying to figure out whether it was a trick question or not, they answered that some said he was John the Baptist, the one to prepare the way for the long-awaited reign of God. Others said he was Elijah who had come back to earth. And still others said he was another good prophet. Then Jesus said, "But who do *you* say I am?"

Peter spoke up. "You are the Christ."

That's right, Christ was not Jesus' last name. The Greek word for "Christ" is *christos*, which means *messiah*. Messiah simply means "anointed one." So Jesus is the savior, the chosen one—the One who will redeem all the brokenness in this world.

Good job, Peter. You stepped up there, bro.

WHAT DID HE SAY ABOUT HIMSELF?

Jesus had some things to say about himself as well. When he calmed the wind and the waves, he declared that he had power over creation. When he took authority over demons, he showed he could control the supernatural.

At the beginning of his ministry, Jesus invited twelve men to follow him as his disciples, which meant he was a Jewish rabbi. In Jesus' time, Jewish culture was kept intact by rabbis and *talmidim*, what we would call teachers

THE GREEK WORD FOR "CHRIST" IS CHRISTOS WHICH MEANS MESSIAH. MESSIAH SIMPLY MEANS ANOINTED ONE.

and disciples. Rabbis who were highly regarded and well respected could walk up to any student of their choosing and say, "Follow me." It meant, "Come be like me. I'm going to teach you to model your life after me." This is exactly what Jesus did, and everyone he said that to knew exactly what he was doing.

The Sabbath was a day of rest, and the Pharisees had created a ton of rules to accompany the Sabbath to ensure that people actually rested. It was illegal not to rest! A person could only take so many steps. No work could be done. No one could work the fields or heal anyone. Even today in Israel, elevators work differently on the Sabbath to ensure limited work. So you can imagine the outrage Jesus caused when he and his disciples picked grain from a field to eat and then healed a man's shriveled hand on the Sabbath. But Jesus didn't stop there. After the religious leaders freaked out, he called himself "Lord of the Sabbath."

Jesus taught in people's homes frequently, and it was usually a packed house, standing room only. One time when was in a home, he heard some men climb onto the roof, dragging something heavy with them. They tore the roof and, as Jesus continued to teach, the men lowered their paralyzed friend into the house, right into the middle of the crowd. Jesus went to the man on the mat and then did the unthinkable. He said, "Your sins are forgiven," which caused another outrage among the religious leaders. Forgiving sins was an action reserved only for God. In forgiving the paralytic, Jesus made the claim that he himself was divine. And to reinforce just how divine he was, Jesus healed the paralyzed man, who picked up his mat and walked out of the house.

And then there was the time Jesus ran into a woman who was drawing water from a well. He asked her for a drink, and the conversation became very personal, very spiritual. Jesus not only discerned some very detailed information about her past relationships, but he also mentioned that if she knew who he was, she would be asking him for a drink of eternal life. Uh oh. He went there. Well, he wasn't done. She said, "I know that Messiah (called Christ) is coming. When he comes, he will explain everything to us" (John 4:25). Basically, she missed what he was saying, so he broke it down even further.

I'll paraphrase for you: "Oh yeah, the Messiah guy you're referring to? That's me."

Mic. Drop.

JESUS KNEW WHO HE WAS AND HE WASN'T SHY ABOUT SAYING IT.

Jesus knew who he was and he wasn't shy about saying it.

ALPHA AND OMEGA, BEGINNING AND END

Reading the last book of the Bible can be a trippy experience, chock-full of brightly colored costumes, fantastical violence, literal future events, imagery, metaphor, and an incredible soundtrack. In an epic showdown between good and evil, Jesus shows up on the scene to put an end to all that's wrong with this world. Throughout the author John's vision in the book of Revelation, we see that both God and Jesus are identified as the first and last, beginning and end, alpha and omega.

In the beginning of John's vision, God is introduced as the alpha and omega, the one who is and who was and who is to come. God existed before anything else, and there will come a time in history when all will see his glory. Just four verses later, Jesus enters the scene. John describes him in all his glory. Dressed as royalty and big enough to hold seven stars in his hands, his voice is as booming as rushing waters. His face is as bright as the sun, with eyes like flames and a sword coming out of his mouth. That's some powerful imagery! And just when John falls to his knees in terror, Jesus tells him not to be afraid because "I am the First and the Last. I am the Living One; I was dead, and now look, I am alive for ever and ever!" (Revelation 1:18). Jesus existed before anything else and will continue after everything else. Jesus was killed, but death could not keep him down.

John's vision continues, complete with signs and wonders and crazy battles. When Jesus wins, a new heaven and earth are established where darkness and evil don't exist anymore. Jesus sits on the throne and lives in community with creation, promising to make all things new. And the king on the throne declares, "It is done. I am the Alpha and Omega, the Beginning and the End" (Revelation 21:6). In the final chapter of Revelation, Jesus encourages us to be ready for his return to make things right with the world and, again, he declares himself alpha, omega, beginning, end, first, and last.

Now, when Jesus calls himself alpha and omega, he's not calling himself the alpha male in the room. He's not the biggest, burliest man doing the most push-ups or leading a pack of wolves. He's not bragging at all. Jesus' claim is something different, something bigger.

Alpha and omega are the first and last letters of the Greek alphabet, so any time we read "I am the al-

JESUS FIRST, JESUS ALWAYS MEANS HE WAS HERE BEFORE YOU GOT HERE AND HE'S GONNA BE HERE AFTER YOU'RE GONE.

THE ULTIMATE TEST OF REAL LOVE IS SACRIFICE.

pha and omega, beginning and end," Jesus is repeating himself. When Jesus calls himself the alpha, first, or beginning, he is saying, "In the beginning there was me. I started it." That means Jesus first. When he calls himself the omega, last, or end, he is saying, "When it's all said and done, I'll finish it." That means Jesus always. Jesus First, Jesus Always means he was here before you got here, and he's gonna be here after you're gone.

But why would he keep saying the same thing multiple times? He doesn't just say it in the first chapter of Revelation. He says it throughout the vision!

The law of repetition

in the Bible is significant. When something is repeated, the author is trying to drive home a point. Jesus is both the beginning and the end, the alpha and omega, the *A* and *Z*. He's also *B, C, D, W, X, Y,* and everything in between.

If Jesus actually is the alpha and omega, first and last, beginning and end—and therefore the point of everything in between—that's a game changer! That means he is literally first. He precedes everything. Not just in priority, but also in eternity.

WHAT DO YOU LOVE?

Remember when I said you could tell a lot about someone by what they love? What did Jesus love? That's quite a question. Right before Jesus was about to die, he spent some time with his disciples, his friends. He talked with them, he washed their feet, and he prayed for them. He encouraged them. He told them something pretty powerful. "My command is this: Love each other as I have loved you. Greater love has no one than this: to lay down one's life for one's friends" (John 15:12–13).

It was one of the last things he told them before he was arrested and crucified. He's telling them to love each other *like he had loved them.* The ultimate test of real love is sacrifice. He was willing to give everything to prove his love for them.

The book of John is one of my favorite books of the Bible. John is so convinced that he is Jesus' favorite disciple that while writing the book he refers to himself as "the disciple whom Jesus loved." I love that so much. I don't think the idea here is that everybody knew John was his favorite—like James says to Luke, "Hey bro, where's Jesus?" and Luke rolls his eyes. "Where do you think? Hanging out with his (air quotes) favorite." No, I believe everyone felt like they were Jesus' favorite. John just had the guts and the passion to say it.

So John is writing this book, and it all starts making sense. Love each other like Jesus loved me. There is no greater love than laying down your life for a friend. Hmm. He did that for me. God so loved the world that he gave his only son. I'm his favorite. He loved me so much. I'm the one he loves. Yes!

See, I'm convinced that if you were to spend any amount of time around Jesus, the love he has for you would be so overwhelming that there would be only one answer to the question, "What does Jesus love more than anything?"

I believe, like John, you would say, "He loves me."

WHO DO YOU SAY I AM?

I had a school assignment once to write a priority list for my life. No further instructions were given. That's a lot of pressure. Have you ever tried to make a priority list for your life? Where do you start? Do you include things you "should" include or the things you actually *want*? If my list included playing *Madden*, watching *Breaking Bad*, eating 4 Rivers Smokehouse barbecue, doing nothing for hours, and chilling by the pool, it wouldn't exactly be a template for world change.

Creating a list based on what you should be doing isn't easy, especially when it comes to Jesus. He doesn't really fit in a Top 10 list alongside family time, cardio, and self-actualization. If he really is who he says he is, then he simply will not fit in as a part of our routine. Why? Because Jesus isn't a line item on an agenda. He is the first and the last, the alpha and the omega, the *A* and the *Z*, which implies that he wants to be everything in between, from start to finish. Jesus is the point of everything, and if he isn't the central plot point in our lives, then we need to adjust our lives to match his.

"Me first, me now, me always" is what eternity looks

like for most people. If I'm not careful, that's the way I will live my life. If I believe that the central plot point of the universe is my own happiness, I'll stop at nothing to ensure that I get exactly what I want.

There are people who say there is no meaning to the beginning of life and no meaning to the end of it. They construct elaborate theories to explain how everything can come from nothing, morality is relative, and randomness caused the world we live in and gave this place the appearance of design. Their platform loudly proclaims the lack of meaning of the beginning and end. The universe began with no purpose, and we will end with no purpose.

But there is a major problem with this train of thought. It is extremely disingenuous and intellectually dishonest to say that the beginning has no meaning and the end has no meaning and then insist that everything in between does have meaning. If both the beginning and the end have no meaning, then the middle has no meaning either.

But we know that our universe and our lives do have meaning. Humans search for purpose our entire lives. Christian or not, we all insist that there must be more than simply existing. Why bother with cardio and eating healthily if it's all for nothing? We all know there is meaning to our lives, and we're desperately doing everything we can to hold on to that meaning or hoping that someday we might find it somewhere.

Keyser Söze is a brilliant character in a movie that amazed audiences with a mind-blowing twist. His identity changed everything we knew about the film. Jesus doesn't make you wait until the end to reveal the truth of who he really is, though. Who he is changes everything.

Who do you say Jesus is? How does your understanding of Jesus impact the way you live? Who has top priority in your life—you or Jesus? Is it possible Jesus might just love you more than you could ever imagine?

IS IT POSSIBLE THAT JESUS MIGHT LOVE YOU MORE THAN YOU COULD EVER IMAGINE?

Right now, how are you living—me first, me always? As we will discover on this journey, there is so much more than that.

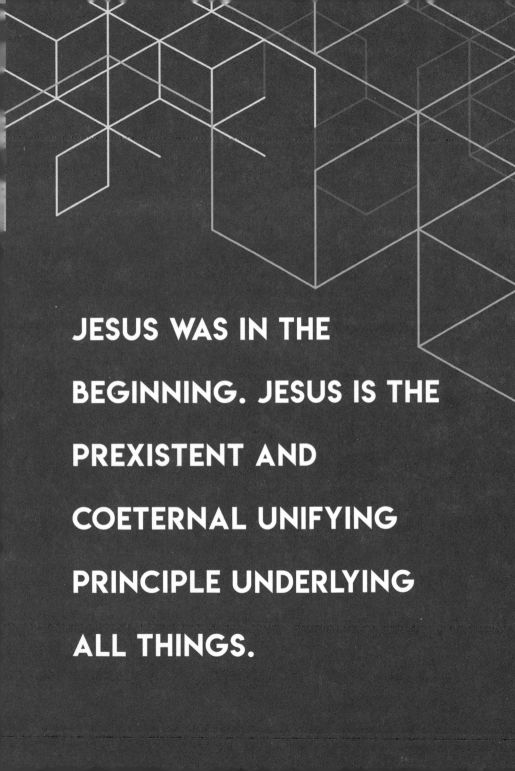

JESUS WAS IN THE BEGINNING. JESUS IS THE PREXISTENT AND COETERNAL UNIFYING PRINCIPLE UNDERLYING ALL THINGS.

CHAPTER TWO:
origin stories

"In the beginning was the Word, and the Word was with God, and the Word was God. He was with God in the beginning. Through him all things were made; without him nothing was made that has been made. In him was life, and that life was the light of all mankind. The light shines in the darkness, and the darkness has not overcome it."

— John 1:1-5

ONCE UPON A TIME

In 1930, when my grandfather was only thirteen, he was a sharecropper in the cotton fields of Alabama. His family had nothing. Sharecroppers rented the land from the owner and split the profits of all the crops. In a few years, Papa Smith joined the U.S. Navy and fought bravely in World War II. When he returned from the war, he had an experience in church, and his whole life changed. He became a small-town pastor. My father was raised in church, and after quite a dramatic path, he eventually became a pastor as well. In 1986, Dad and Mom started the church I now pastor. In just a few years it grew from twenty-five people to several thousand, more than twenty acres, and big buildings everywhere. It was unlike anything my family had ever been used to.

My grandfather eventually moved to Florida, and he would sit on the back row of our church and look around with the biggest smile on his face, in awe of the whole thing. He would point to the buildings and say, "I just don't understand how all this happened." Then we'd laugh together. It's pretty amazing what can happen in just a few generations. I guess to some degree that's my origin story.

It's always fun to know someone's origin story. It seems like right now Americans are fascinated, even obsessed, with them. Almost every comic book character is getting a spin-off these days.

I'm kind of partial to *Batman Begins*. And Wolverine has how many movies? Comics publish multiple backstories because they make the big bucks. *Wicked*, the famous book and Broadway production, tells how Galinda became Glinda the Good Witch and Elphaba became the Wicked Witch of the West. Harry Potter fans freaked out when they learned the new Harry Potter play wasn't a prequel with the much-beloved cast of characters. We want to know all the juicy details that help us fill in the gaps.

We love this stuff! But it's not anything new. Humans have always wanted to know origin stories. The

HUMANS HAVE ALWAYS WANTED TO KNOW ORIGIN STORIES.

famous "Where do babies come from?" question is universal. By the way, props to the guy who invented the stork answer! I like that. A bird, a big bird—that's where they come from. He's probably thinking, "By the time this poor child possesses enough logic to know how implausible this is, they will probably have figured out the answer on their own and will be too embarrassed to confront me about it." Our family took a direct, proactive approach to this question, and while I am thankful for the openness in our family, it would have been much easier to say, "A big bird." But I digress . . .

Sociology is the study of human origins and development. We've turned our origin stories into high-school subjects. History is the study of past events. We can't know how we got here without understanding our history. Societies have erected statues and monuments to remind us of our history, our origins. The Israelites piled up rocks at famous battle sites and places where God had helped them along their journey. The Egyptians built pyramids to house their dead leaders. Go to Washington, DC, and I guarantee you'll get a history lesson visiting the monuments.

People have identified signs in nature that remind us of our stories. When we see a rainbow, we're reminded of

GOD'S WORD BRINGS LIFE, ORDER, AND HOPE TO THE ENTROPY AND DISCORD.

God's promise not to flood the earth. Holidays surround the changing of seasons. Christmas reminds us of Jesus' birth, and Easter reminds us of his resurrection. Jews celebrate Passover to remember when God brought them out of Egypt. All origin stories.

All civilizations have attempted to explain the beginnings of creation and humanity. While some of the explanations may sound familiar, others seem to come out of left field. The Kotas, an ancient Nilgiri tribe in India, believed that the original tribes of their people came from the god Kamataraya's sweat droplets. Mayans believed that the gods Kukulkán and Tepeu unsuccessfully created man out of mud, then wood. After trial and error, they ended up settling on the corniest idea yet: maize. The Native American Yuchi tribe believed that in the beginning, water covered everything, and when asked who would bring forth land, Sock-chew, the crawfish, volunteered. Sock-chew the Crawfish kicked off human history.

IN THE BEGINNING, GOD . . .

The biblical creation account is beautiful and moving. There is a formless void, and God's preexistent, eternal Spirit moves over the chaos. God's very word causes light to explode though the darkness. It brings life, order, and hope to the entropy and discord. Galaxies and stars are born. Governance is brought to the earth as God appoints the moon and stars to light up the night sky and the sun to rule the day. They became signs for seasons, days, and years. He created every plant and every living creature uniquely.

Finally, he moves on to his most important creation. God formed man out of his own image. Any artist considers a self-portrait to be an incredibly personal work. God is no different. He sculpted man from a lump of clay the way a child plays with Play-Doh® and breathed life into him. He decided man shouldn't be alone (great call), so God caused him to go into a deep sleep, and while he slept, God took one of his ribs and fashioned his counterpart, woman. When the man awoke from his slumber, he rubbed the sleep from his eyes, and before him was what he had been longing for: Catherine-Zeta Jones in *Zorro*. A woman to be his companion—similar to himself, yet so maddeningly different. He knew at this very moment that he would never win an argument again. But he was cool with that.

The creation narrative tells us a story that illustrates a compelling truth about God and humans. God created the cosmos, yet paid special enough attention to humans that he crafted his very own image into us all. But that's not the whole story. Humanity's real story rests within God's larger creative and redemptive story for all of creation. And we learn that in the first phrase of the Bible. "In the beginning, when God created . . ." God already existed. God was already there before anything else.

SO . . . WHAT ABOUT JESUS?

We've already established that Jesus is the Alpha, Omega,

beginning, and end. So how does he fit within our origin story? If Jesus was there in the beginning, where was he? What was his role? The early Christians who established the Nicene Creed had the right idea. Jesus was part of the creative process, not a creation. Jesus was preexistent and coeternal with God. But how did they come to that conclusion?

Revelation isn't the first time in the Bible when we read that Jesus was there in the beginning. The first chapter of John adds to our Genesis creation story. It begins with a poetic illustration about God's creative action: "in the beginning was the Word, and the Word was

JESUS WAS PART OF THE CREATIVE PROCESS, NOT A CREATION.

with God, and the Word was God." Wait. What?

How can the Word be *with* God, but also *be* God? How in the world do we know who the Word is, and what does that even mean? And what does that *passage* even mean?!

John 1 goes on to identify the Word as the one who took on flesh and lived in the world. Hmm, a clue. It tells us that the Word, whoever or whatever it was, is the one who created everything around us in the beginning. "Through him all things were made; without him nothing was made that has been made" (John 1:3). Sounds like the confusing Beatles line. "There's nothing you can make that can't be made."

In the beginning was the Word. You say, "What kind of name is 'the Word?' Who calls themselves 'the Word?'" See, John wasn't using some weird, esoteric name no one understood. In Greek, the word for "word" is *logos*, but the English translation is really poor. In our modern Western thought, the term "word" refers to spoken communication, but that's not all that *logos* means in Greek.

In Greek philosophy, *logos* was the unifying principle underlying all things, the orderly account of all that existed. In first century Rome, *logos* wasn't a word that made people ask, "What's that?" No, no, no. In their culture it meant, "This is the answer and meaning behind every-thing in life." It means something far beyond all of our concepts of God. *Logos* is the ultimate answer for every-thing. Kind of like how "Jesus" is the correct answer for almost any Sunday school question.

John 1 says the Word was the creative force at the very beginning. Through the Word every living creature came into being. The laws of physics were written by the Word, the *logos*. Creation happened through the *logos*. The expansion of the universe continues through the *logos*. The atoms forming molecules, which formed stars and planets and galaxies, happened through the *logos*. Our tiny little planet was fashioned through the ultimate creative force that organizes the building blocks of our universe—the *logos*. From the very beginning, along with God, the *logos* was there. And John goes on to identify the *logos* as the one who took on flesh—Jesus. Jesus was in the beginning. Jesus is the *logos*, the preexistent and coeternal unifying princi-ple underlying all things.

When John said, "In the beginning was the *logos*," he was saying, "I knew this guy." He's the beginning of all things. He thought of all this. He executed all of it. He's the purpose behind it all.

That's why Jesus says, "I am the very beginning of all things. I started all this. I created all this. All this was created for me. It's by me. It's all about me. My fingerprints are everywhere. The trees outside swaying in the wind are actually lifting their hands to give honor and praise to me. The rocks you think you're just walking on every day, they'll cry out to me if you don't. That's how much this universe points to me!"

John goes on to say, "The Word became flesh and blood, and moved into the neighborhood" (John 1:14, MSG). What? The Supreme Answer for the Universe? Living in *my* 'hood? That

JESUS WAS IN THE BEGINNING. JESUS IS THE LOGOS, THE PREEXISTENT AND COETERNAL UNIFYING PRINCIPLE UNDERLYING ALL THINGS.

might be one of the coolest verses ever. Jesus isn't just God's long-lost Son, some figure hanging on a cross in a church somewhere, or somebody's homeboy. He is God. He made all this.

"In the beginning was *Jesus*, and *Jesus* was with God, and *Jesus* was God. He was in the beginning with God. Through him all things were made; without him nothing was made that has been made. In him was life, and that life was the light of all mankind. The light shines in the darkness, and the darkness has not overcome it" (John 1:1-5, emphasis mine). Jesus is the Alpha, the Omega, the *logos*, the creative force behind all we see in this universe. That's one heck of an origin story.

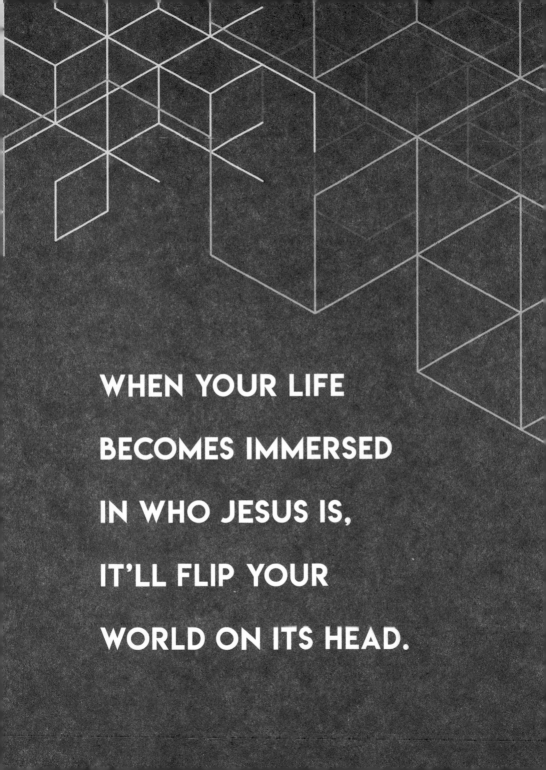

WHEN YOUR LIFE
BECOMES IMMERSED
IN WHO JESUS IS,
IT'LL FLIP YOUR
WORLD ON ITS HEAD.

CHAPTER THREE:
more than a motto

"Well done is better than well said."

— **Benjamin Franklin**[1]

ME FIRST, ME ALWAYS

When I married my wife, Amy, I was twenty-nine years old. Like the incredibly sensitive man I've always wanted to be, I laid down the ground rules, the non-negotiables. Rule number one: Never schedule anything on the weekends during football season. Ever. We had dated for six years, and she knew my habits well, but for some reason I felt the need to make this the eleventh commandment. Amy loves football, so she was very sweet about it. She would find ways to schedule things that didn't interfere with weekends. She was amazing.

She didn't come into our marriage with a list of

demands; she just loved me. After a while this became clear to me. It made me want to just love her. I started suggesting that we do other things, even on the days of big games, and though she was shocked, I could see how much it meant to her. Something happened. I began to realize the power of putting someone else before myself. The more I preferred her, the more she wanted to prefer me. I never realized how selfish I'd been my whole life until Amy showed me so much kindness, even when I was a jerk.

This whole situation was actually a big turning point for me because I realized it paralleled several areas of my life where I was happy helping others, or even loving God, as long as it didn't infringe on what I really wanted. I had lived most of my life putting myself first.

UNFOLLOWED

I'll never forget the day I logged onto my Facebook account and saw a notification that "Amy Smith wants to be your friend." I thought, "How nice—my wife finally wants to be my friend!" Then my dad added me soon after. What a world we live in. We can be friends with our family members in real life but not be "Facebook official." That's how you know a dating relationship is serious these days.

Then Twitter came out, and you could "follow" someone. You didn't even have to know someone to follow them. It was socially acceptable stalking. It's the same for Instagram, Vine, Snapchat, and whatever the next up-and-coming social media platform may be.

It's a great feeling when someone adds you as a friend or follower, but have you ever felt what it's like to be unfriended or unfollowed? And it's even worse when that person tries to friend you back again, like you forgot that they dropped you already. You get a second chance everywhere in life *except* Facebook. As much as it stings to be unfriended or unfollowed, if that's ever happened to you, you're in good company because Jesus was unfriended—on a massive scale.

Jesus got unfollowed.

As Jesus' early ministry was growing, he had such a large posse following his miracles and healings that he withdrew up a mountain with his close circle of twelve. Apparently, the crowds didn't catch the hint or have any sense of personal space because when Jesus looked up, there they were, climbing up that mountain.

As they approached, Jesus asked Philip where they were going to buy all the bread for the crowds to have a meal. They were a long way from a local market, but Philip didn't really care about where they were going to get the bread. His question was *how*? How were they going to pay for all that bread? 5,000 people were climbing a mountain to hear Jesus talk, and that much food is not cheap. I can appreciate Philip's mind for logistics because six months' wages wouldn't have bought enough bread to feed the crowd even just a little bit.

But the fisherman-disciple Andrew noticed a little boy carrying five loaves of bread and two fish. Now we know fishermen weren't especially well-educated during that time, but come on. Five loaves and two fish? The average loaf of bread is a foot long and half a foot tall and deep. Divide that out among 5,000 people, and each person would have gotten a pinch of bread, half an inch large. Communion crackers are bigger than that.

But when Jesus had the crowd sit down, he took the five loaves of bread and two fish, blessed it, and passed the meager meal around. Every single person ate their fill, and there were leftovers. A bite-sized snack turned into a

WHEN JESUS IS FIRST AND ALWAYS, OUR SPIRITUAL HUNGER AND THIRST IS SATISFIED.

Thanksgiving feast.

Everyone present failed to realize that they were being set up for a greater revelation. The disciples collected *twelve baskets full* of leftovers. That's more than they started with. The following day, after Jesus and his disciples had already moved on to Capernaum, some of the people among the crowds followed him. They begged for more bread and more signs that Jesus was from God. He replied, "I am the bread of life. Whoever comes to me will never go hungry, and whoever believes in me will never be thirsty" (John 6:35).

Never be hungry or thirsty again? I'm in.

But they didn't understand what he actually meant. Jesus wasn't saying they'd never have to eat food or drink liquids again. He was saying that when we feast on Jesus, when we *ingest* Jesus, when Jesus is *first* and *always*, our spiritual hunger and thirst is satisfied.

Feast on Jesus? Eat his flesh and drink his blood? That's offensive. That's scandalous. It's gross. People would have preferred him to go back to doing cool tricks and giving them free food.

It was so radical, actually, that a lot of people clicked "unfollow." John 6:66 is one of the saddest verses ever to me: "many of his disciples turned back and no longer followed him."

The day after they witnessed a miracle, they just couldn't do it anymore. They thought Jesus was going Hannibal Lecter on everyone.

Sometimes I hear this scripture and think, *I understand the crowd leaving. The crowds are just in it for the spectacle.* But it says in verse 66 that many of his disciples—not just fans, not just spectators—but many of his *disciples* turned back and followed him no longer.

I guess the reason that's so shocking to me is the idea of what a disciple really meant in the first century. A disciple was called a *talmid* (not the Talmud which is the collection of Jewish writings), a pupil who had submitted his entire life to the master teacher. The master teacher, the rabbi, would have been the best of the best—the Leonardo da Vinci of Jewish religion—and the *talmidim* (plural for *talmid*) would have submitted their lives to the teacher. The goal was not just to learn from, acquire the knowledge of, or pass the class of the teacher. The goal was to become *exactly like the teacher.*

That's what that whole relationship was based on. The goal was to become like the teacher. They would follow the rabbi everywhere, sometimes even to the bathroom. I love people, but mentorship needs limits.

When John 6:66 tells us that many disciples left Jesus, it's intense. The ones who had submitted their lives to him abandoned him. The ones who had committed to becoming like Jesus heard something he said and clicked the unfriend button. They clicked the Unfollow button in their lives. And the minute they clicked that button, the truth was out. They wanted to cherry-pick the things they liked and disliked about Jesus, the things they'd accept and the things they wouldn't.

But, let's face it, they aren't the only ones.

We like to cherry-pick Jesus, too. We want to form our own ideas about what faith in Jesus looks like. Like playing with Mr. Potatohead, we take what we like, and we put that on top of, around, and all over Jesus, making him look the way we want him to look, sound the way we think he should sound, and ultimately, into something less than he really is. That's not in line with having no other gods before the true God, the first commandment. It's not even close. That's creating a god that suits your own preferences.

But then suddenly, in John 6, Jesus says, "I am the bread of life. You have to eat my flesh and drink my blood if you want any part of me." He's saying that everything he is—his love and goodness and mercy and justice, the moral principles he stands for—you must take and put it inside you. It must become every part of who you are, your heart. We must let his life transform our lives from head to toe. And so, people thought, *I don't really know if I like that*. Even some of his disciples questioned it. "Hey, Jesus, eat your flesh and drink your blood? I mean, I'm your dude, but can't you come up with a different analogy? I love you, but that sounds a little bit cray."

Jesus says, "Nah. Eat my flesh, drink my blood.

That's what I said. I won't soften it or change it. It's not gonna be easy to follow me."

Click.

When we're fair-weather fans in our faith, we're saying that the cost of following Jesus does not fit our personal preferences. We find someone or something else to follow.

I believe there were two groups of disciples at that time. There were students who listened to what the teacher had to say and obeyed the rules so they could pass the class. That's what a lot of students do. They follow everything to a T in order to get the grade. They commit things to memory temporarily to pass the test, but they can never remember them again. I believe this was the group who unfollowed Jesus.

But a different group of people stayed with Jesus. After many of the disciples left him, Jesus looked at his closest friend, Peter, and asked, "Are you leaving me too?" But Peter was different than the others. He wasn't just a fly-by-night follower. He was a *talmid*. He didn't just want to pass the test. He wanted to be like the teacher. So to him, leaving wasn't an option. His response? "But to whom would I go?"

WHEN YOUR LIFE BECOMES IMMERSED IN WHO JESUS IS, IT'LL FLIP YOUR WORLD ON ITS HEAD.

For Peter, Jesus was first, and Jesus was always. Jesus was the Alpha and Omega, and the *logos*. Peter had submitted his life to Jesus. When faced with the option of leaving, he didn't even have a plan B.

For *talmidim*, becoming like their teacher wasn't a priority or a motto. It was life. Jesus' disciples fashioned their lives after him rather than putting him on a priority list. Jesus First, Jesus Always is more than a motto. Living like a *talmid* changes everything. When your life becomes immersed in who Jesus is, it'll flip your world on its head.

A true *talmid* wants to be like the teacher. A true *talmid* seeks intimacy with his rabbi so he can model the life of his rabbi. A true *talmid* doesn't leave her rabbi when the rabbi doesn't fit her personal preferences.

"Who do you say I am?" That's the question Jesus asked his *talmidim* after many had unfollowed him. He was asking where he fit into their lives. Was he just a part of what they did and said? Did he just say things they had to memorize? Or was he something more?

What is the focus of your life—the *real* focus? Not the one you tell your boss, or your friends, or even the one you tell yourself. Most Christians want to say, "Jesus," but have you considered the cost of being Jesus' *talmid*? Have you weighed the concept of making Jesus the central plot point of your world? Have you taken into account the idea that he will desire things that will be contrary to everything you want at any given moment of your life, and yet you will submit your will to his anyway? Most of us have not, if we're honest with ourselves.

Following Jesus doesn't fit when we're living a me first, me always life. When we try to be the beginning, the end, and everything in between, there's no room for becoming a talmid. We can try to fit Jesus into our world, but we'll just get frustrated when things don't work out.

Jesus First, Jesus Always. We don't need another hashtag. We don't need another motto. What we need is a heart revelation that becomes a soul revolution. This revelation has everything to do with who you believe Jesus is. Is he first? Is he last? Is he everything in between?

Follow or unfollow? Your choice.

Either Jesus is your first, always, and everything in between, or you are. Jesus doesn't play the game of thrones.

FIRST, BEFORE POSSESSIONS

Since it was such an extreme commitment to become a talmid, Jesus made sure people knew what they were getting themselves into before they signed their lives away. The commitment wasn't just a one-time prayer, and then they were good for the rest of their lives. It was a lifelong journey and the pursuit of becoming like Jesus. When people came to Jesus half-heartedly without weighing the cost, he called them out. He gave them an opportunity to really think about what they were saying.

In Luke 9, Jesus encountered three people who just didn't get it. He had interactions with three wannabe disciples, but he showed them that their motives were not pure. They hadn't really thought about what it meant to be a disciple.

"Then he and his disciples went to another village. As they were walking along the road, a man said to him, 'I will follow you wherever you go'" (Luke 9:56–57). That sounds so lovely, doesn't it? It sounds like exactly the kind of person Jesus would want to meet—a guy who says, "Jesus, I'm 100% in. I will go *wherever you go*." Jesus is thinking, *Okay, well I'm about to go to the cross. I'm about to be beaten to a pulp where no one can tell whether I'm a man or a woman. I'm going there. You're going to go wherever I go? Okay. I'm going to be mocked. I'm going to be scorned. I'm going to go through persecution. They're going to hang me on a tree, and I'm going to die. I am going to take on the sins of all of humankind, but you're going to go wherever I go. Thank you, man. I really appreciate that.*

Jesus responds to this man in a shocking way that cuts to the heart. Essentially, he says, "Well, number one, I see it in your heart that you love your life too much. You love your house too much. You love your sofa too much. You love your 70-inch flat screen television too much. You like the comforts of life way too much to be telling me that you're willing to go wherever I go."

This is what Jesus *actually* said: "Foxes have dens and birds have nests, but the Son of Man has no place to lay his head" (Luke 9:58). So if you want to follow him, you've got to be willing to lay down every comfort in your life, every possession you love. It doesn't mean that when you become a Christian you'll never have another possession or any comfort. It means that you have to lay it all down because you may not ever have more. Jesus is telling us, "Man, if you've never thought about that, then don't just tickle my ears or fool yourself by telling me that you'll follow me wherever I go. You haven't even weighed out what it might cost. You're not even willing to give up your home."

The comforts of life cannot come before Jesus. It sounds trite, but we get this wrong so many times. In the back of our minds we say, "Okay, I could serve Jesus as long as I've got this lifestyle and as long as I've got this car . . . at least a house that I'm comfortable with and at least this and at least that." We're not understanding that Jesus called us to a life of simply loving him. That's it—regardless of our circumstances, possessions, comforts, or discomforts. He wants to be the everything in our life, and life becomes so wonderful and fulfilling when he does.

Jesus said, "I am the way, the truth, and the life" (John 14:6). It's interesting that he refers to himself as the *way* and not the *destination*. So many people think of Jesus as a one-way ticket to heaven when they die, but he's not talking about where he's taking you. He says, "I am the *way*." Jesus is the way of life. This whole journey of giving up ourselves is part of the life Jesus calls us to. What you learn about Jesus is that he is the way, but the way *is* the destination.

FIRST, BEFORE RESPONSIBILITIES

After the first man, Jesus encounters another and invites him to be a disciple. Once again, not just casual language. He's calling this man to the life of a *talmid*, to model his life after him. He's inviting him. *Come on, let me show you the way to live. Follow me. Emulate me. Be like me in everything I do.* The guy responds, "Oh, oh, yeah, yeah. Jesus, that's good. I want to follow you and everything, but first . . ."

. . . but first.

Okay, for real, do you think Jesus is going to have that today? Do you think he's going to have that *any* day? We come up with all kinds of excuses we think no one could argue with. This guy comes up with a pretty good one. "Yeah, no, totally. I want to follow you. You are amazing. You're awesome. I love you. I've been following you for a while. I heard about what you did with the bread and the people. That was the best. I want to be your disciple, totally interested in that. But first, let me go bury my father."

Who's going to argue with that?

So it appears that his dad is dead, but that's probably not the case here. In Jewish culture, many people had fathers who were about to pass their businesses on to them, control of the family, things of that nature. People often referred to it in the *future* tense. "Let me go bury my father" meant that his dad was getting old. We don't know when he was going to die—maybe a year, maybe two years, maybe further down the road—but he was in the process of getting his family affairs in order. He was saying that once his dad died, he received his inheritance, and his future was a little clearer to him, *at that point* he'd be willing to follow Jesus.

Now, how many of us have done that same thing with some area of our life? We say, "Oh, Jesus, of course, I want to follow you. You are amazing. I can't wait to do it. I'm totally into this, but just let me graduate high school first because I have lots of things on my plate right now." Or we say, "Oh, but of course, I love you. I love going to church. I love singing to you. I even give to you and all that stuff, but I'm in college right now. It's really tough, but I'm doing all this for you. If you just give me a little bit." Or, "I'm going to, but just let me get through the terrible two's, Jesus. It's so tough with the kids. They're opening cabinets everywhere and about to drink pesticides. It's just hard to deal with all that stuff with these babies. They won't listen. You know how it is, but I'm doing it for you."

First, let me go bury my father. First let me do this. First let me do that. But Jesus answers him (and us) when he says, "Let the dead bury the dead."

But I thought Jesus was compassionate?!

Oh, he's got a lot of compassion. His compassion gives us fair warning. "If you're not ready for this, don't jump into it and get disillusioned and turn away from me forever because you can't handle it. Weigh it out first. Let the spiritually dead bury their dead. If you don't understand the significance of how much you need me right now, you probably never will."

Then he says, "But as for you, go and proclaim the kingdom of God. Follow me now."

Don't worry about getting all your ducks in a row first. Now is the time. There's never going to be a time for anyone to follow Jesus like right now. Sometimes people even try to work out moral issues in their lives before they will follow Jesus. In essence, Jesus is saying that the way you work out issues is by coming to him to begin with. You don't have to put one thing in order to follow Jesus right now. As a matter of fact, Jesus will put things in order *for* you when you begin to follow him.

FIRST, BEFORE RELATIONSHIPS

Next person. Still another said, "I will follow you, Lord. But first—" Here we go, another creative thinker. Believe me. I've tried all these angles in some way or another myself. He's got a good one here. No one would ever rebut such a heartwarming request. "But first let me go back and say goodbye to my family." Finally, someone has stumped the master. Uh, bro, meet Jesus.

Jesus fires back and says that no one who follows him and looks back at what's left behind is even fit for the Kingdom of God. Ouch.

Jesus gets right to business. The first person Jesus deals with illustrates that possessions can't come before Jesus. The second person shows us that responsibilities can't come before Jesus. Now, with this third person, we're realizing that relationships can't come before Jesus.

But it's not that Jesus wants to be top priority. When you become a disciple of Jesus, it's not Jesus, then your family. It's not Jesus, then your job. It's not Jesus, then your kids. This is a conversation about the infusion of who Jesus is *into everything you are*. This is atomic. It's architectural. It's substructural. This is guts.

We are invited to come *now* to Jesus. We have to come with everything we have. Our

WE HAVE TO COME WITH EVERYTHING WE HAVE. OUR POSSESSSIONS, RESPONSIBILITIES, AND RELATIONSHIPS CAN'T COME FIRST.

possessions can't come first. Our responsibilities can't come first. Our relationships can't come first. We have to come to Jesus right now and say, "I'm going to follow you. I want to be like you. I don't want to just say what you say and do what you do. I want to know why you do it. I want to know everything you are. I want to be exactly like you." That's what a *talmid*, a disciple, is all about. That's the life we're meant to live.

Jesus First, Jesus Always is a way of life in which Jesus is infused into every facet of life—no compartmentalization, not just a top priority; he is the underlying principle by which you live. We all have lists of the things that

CENTER YOUR LIFE IN THE MIDDLE OF WHO JESUS IS, RATHER THAN TRYING TO PUT HIM IN THE CENTER OF WHAT YOU DO.

seem important to us, but frankly, Jesus is bigger and better than all of it. Jesus came before you, and he's going to be here after you're gone. And if you choose to live within that reality, anything you do is going to fit in between everything Jesus is. Center your life in the middle of who Jesus is, rather than trying to put him in the center of what you do.

THE BIG EVENT

I had a friend, a close friend, who weighed this out, and he lived it in the face of unimaginable adversity. He was tempted to walk away when Jesus' message didn't fit his personal preferences. It would have been very easy to click unfollow when Jesus' teachings were too hard, but he didn't. His faith transformed the way I see myself and the way I seek Jesus. What happened to him, what he did, and how he followed Jesus will forever be an example to me, and the challenge he faced is one of the things that led me to write this book.

Dave was not just my friend; he was one of the best friends I've ever had. He was very smart and graduated high school at sixteen. I offered him a job as a video editor, and as the years went by, I taught him how to play music, write songs, and give a message to an audience. He eventually took over as the youth pastor of our church. He was a natural leader. He never missed a meeting, was always on time, and always spent time with people who might otherwise get overlooked. I could always count on Dave to do something and do it well.

Dave got married, and shortly afterward, he and his wife, Sheena, found out they were having a little girl. By that time, Dave and I had become the best of friends; he was my bro. We laughed at the most esoteric things, we dreamed huge dreams, and he wanted to be my right-hand guy no matter what we did.

One night he called me while I was writing. He said, "I really need to talk to you." I closed my laptop immediately because I had never heard him sound like that. He told me he'd been diagnosed with metastatic thymic carcinoma, a rare form of cancer only seen a few other times in history. There had never been a successful treatment. At the age of twenty-five, he basically told me he was dying.

I'd like to tell you that my faith was strong, and I didn't flinch. That would be a lie because I was devastat-

ed. The next eighteen months ended up being the tough-
est of my life.

I had recently taught a series at my church called
"The Life You Were Meant to Live." When Dave asked
if I would help him get through his trial by writing a book
together based on that theme, I agreed. I would have done
anything to encourage him or help him feel a sense of
purpose in the midst of his darkest moments.

We decided Dave would send me a weekly recording
of how he felt after chemo and radiation treatments. He
would record himself being honest about his thought process, not holding anything back, and I would write about
it. Neither of us knew what we were in for.

Dave had such a deep love for Jesus. His voice would
quiver as he wondered out loud about the cause of his
condition. Was it his fault? Was he good enough? Did Jesus love him as much as other people who have recovered
from terrible diseases? At times, it was nearly impossible
for me to listen to his pain, but he pressed on with such
purpose that I had to go on. He always would say, "Maybe
this will help somebody who feels like I do."

His daughter, Sydney, was born. He felt guilty for not
being able to be the kind of father and husband he wanted

to be. He was losing weight rapidly, and his appearance had completely changed. Weeks would go by with no recordings because he got too weak to even speak. One day he called and said, "I feel really good today. It's really strange. I have a lot of energy." I asked if I could bring my camera to his house and film some of the material we had been working on. Once that camera began to roll, he looked into it and spoke with a heart-wrenching desperation.

"Hi, my name is Dave. I'm a husband, I'm a dad, I'm a son, I'm a friend. I'm also a pastor. I thought I had life pretty much all figured out a couple of years ago. Everything was going good. I had just gotten married, had a baby on the way and a great job. I loved getting out of bed every day. There was really nothing more I wanted. And then, something happened, something changed. I got a phone call, and the voice simply said, 'You have cancer.' That was a difficult night. I couldn't even tell my wife. I left the house, just trying to come to terms with it myself and say it out loud. It took so long for me to say it out loud. I just couldn't get it out . . . 'I have cancer.'

"My perspective of life really changed. The things that mattered the day before didn't matter so much. The things I'd get upset about before I didn't really care about now. The things I valued I valued so much more now than before. I'd see people going through their days and wonder, 'Do they really know how nice it would be to just walk down the street?'

"I felt tortured with a question. Do I love God more than my health? Something in my mind told me if I just said, 'I love my health more,' then I'd be healed. I wanted to say it so bad. It took me some time to answer, but through prayer and knowing what he has brought me through, I couldn't lie to myself. I know I love God more. I don't get to trade. I don't get a different life. It puts such value on every day.

HOW MUCH TIME DO WE WASTE NOT SAYING THE THINGS WE REALLY MEAN OR NOT DOING THE THINGS WE REALLY WANT TO DO?

"How much time do we waste not saying the things we really mean or not doing the things we really want to do? Or how often do we wait for something to happen in our life that'll make us change? Well, we're not guaranteed that day or that time. It could all change today, tomorrow, tonight. No one knows. Don't wait for that big event in your life. This is the event. I have cancer, but I'm trusting God no matter how it feels. Look at me for one second. I want you to remember my face. If anything I've said has touched you, if it challenges you to change your life the way you are supposed to, then everything I've been through is worth it."

Dave passed away a few weeks later.

He struggled with fear like any of us do. He struggled with motives like any of us do. Ultimately, though, he put nothing, even in his own heart, in front of Jesus. It might be difficult to see someone be honest about the way we really live life. Sometimes it takes someone in Dave's condition to see the truth for what it is. David was confronted with whether his own life was more important than Jesus. Are we strong enough to confront ourselves with these questions today? Are we honest enough to assess this kind of brutal truth whether we are facing a life-or-death situation or not? Having known some of the things Dave went through, I feel a personal responsibility to search my heart on a daily basis and answer the tough questions. Do I love Jesus more than my family? Do I love Jesus more than my health? Heck, do I even love Jesus more than random desires at any given moment? The answer to these questions is found in the way we live our lives, and most of the time the answer is, sadly, no.

When it really comes down to it, who is first in your life—you or Jesus? Do you recognize that Jesus is first in pre-existence? Do you honor that idea with the way you live, or do you live as if the universe comes after you? Do you recognize that Jesus is first in priority? Do you honor that idea with the way you live, or does the world revolve around you? Do you recognize that Jesus *precedes* you?

Say this out loud, and then pray this with a sincere heart:

> *Jesus precedes me. Jesus is first in pre-existence,*
> *Jesus is first in priority.*

If you meant that, something is about to change in your life.

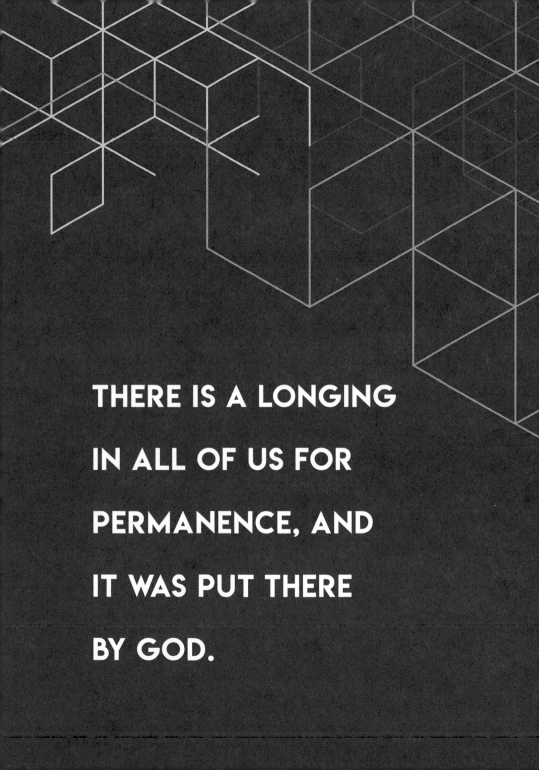

THERE IS A LONGING
IN ALL OF US FOR
PERMANENCE, AND
IT WAS PUT THERE
BY GOD.

CHAPTER FOUR:
always

Not   for   just   an   hour,
Not   for   just   a   day,
Not   for   just   a   year,
But   always.
—**Irving Berlin**[2]

THE BODYGUARD

Always.

That is a massive word.

Whitney Houston sold twelve million copies of the single "I Will Always Love You" because the idea of always, while a bit overwhelming, resonates with something inside all of us. When it comes to the most vital needs of human beings, we don't want *sometimes*, we want *always*. Food? Always. Shelter? Always. Love? Always. Acceptance? Always. Great abs? Get the point?

SO HOW DO WE RECONCILE THE NEED FOR PERMANENCE AND THE HESITANCY WE FEEL ABOUT COMMITTING TO IT?

Though we long for always, sometimes we're not very good at keeping our end of the bargain to make it happen. The tattoo removal industry wouldn't be so prolific if we were good at making always happen. Always can be as intimidating as it is inviting. I don't even like to sign a two-year phone contract. I feel trapped. I know lots of people who are in love and could get married, but they are afraid of always.

So how do we reconcile the need for permanence and the hesitancy we feel about committing to it?

Jesus knows that we're not very good at keeping commitments. He is. Deuteronomy 31:8 in *The Message* says it perfectly: "God is striding ahead of you. He's right there with you. He won't let you down; he won't leave you. Don't be intimidated. Don't worry."

This says everything about Jesus' character, not ours. When I fail, he's there. When I miss the point, he's there. When I'm hurting, he's there. When I throw my golf club in front of two church members, he's there. When it comes to our relationship with Jesus, always has way more to do with his love than ours. Why? Because he knows we will fail him, but he loves us anyway.

THE SMOKING FIRE POT AND FLAMING TORCH

In Genesis 15 God is talking to Abram (later known as Abraham), promising him incredible blessings. Even though Abram knows these blessings are God's favor and mercy, and even though the only thing he's been credited for is his faith, God still instructs Abram to bring some animals and cut them in half in order to arrange a covenant ceremony to seal the deal. I understand this sounds wild, but it was a common ritual. After the animals were cut in half, the pieces were laid out with a path between the halves. The two parties walked between the pieces and recited the oath, "If I do not fulfill the terms of this cove-nant, may the destruction that befell these animals also be upon my head," essentially bringing a curse upon them-selves if they failed to keep their responsibilities.

Abram falls asleep and sees the craziest thing. "When the sun had set and darkness had fallen, a smoking firepot with a blazing torch appeared and passed between the pieces" (Genesis 15:17).

Though this may sound like a missing Harry Potter book, it's bigger than you can imagine. A theophany—a visible manifestation of God—takes place. God appeared as a flame of fire to the children of Israel in the wilder-ness. Here he's a smoking firepot with a flaming torch. We are told that on Mount Sinai God's presence was covering the mountain with smoke and fire. This is a representation of the very presence of God.

But God doesn't require Abram to go between the pieces with him in the traditional way. He goes between the pieces alone. Do you see what's happening? Abram doesn't participate in the covenant ritual; he watches it.

The blessing promised to the now-Abraham be-longs to us now. God keeps both ends of the deal himself. Without getting too deep, God previews Jesus' death on the cross, fulfilling our end of the deal. Though man can never fulfill God's commands, Jesus becomes a man and fulfills them all, yet suffers the very punishment foreshadowed here. God was saying, "I am going to bless you and be with you and prosper you, and if I don't, may my fate be as the fate of these animals." It happened. He sacrificed himself on the cross to pay the price for the collective sins of humanity. Now we are required to simply come to God with faith. He kept the rest of the deal himself.

I don't know about you, but I think that is pretty encouraging.

NEVER ALONE

What if we mess up? Do we lose out on the blessings? Will Jesus get mad at us and leave us if we can't get our act together? These are reasonable questions with an extraordinary answer.

Part of Jesus' character is revealed to us in Scripture before he was even born. "Therefore the Lord himself will give you a sign: The virgin will conceive and give birth to a son, and will call him Immanuel" (Isaiah 7:14).

Immanuel means "God with us."

Jesus not only came to live among us long ago; he's

here to stay today.

When I was a teenager I was in our church building way past midnight one night writing a song. My studio was upstairs, and I came down into the dark empty sanctuary while I was on the way to my car. I was still singing the song out loud, and the acoustics sounded really cool. I went up to the stage and started singing the song as if the room were packed with people. I was telling the imaginary people to lift their hands and sing with all their might. I finished the song and heard a voice say, "Nice song," from deep within the darkness. If accidentally cussing in a church sent one to hell, I'd be in trouble.

WHEN IT HURTS, WHEN YOU FEEL BROKEN, AND WHEN YOU FEEL ABANDONED, YOU ARE NOT ALONE.

I screamed and fell to the floor in fear. My dad was sitting on the back row praying when I had walked in. He thought it would be funny to sit and watch me perform. I apologized profusely as he sat and laughed in tears. I thought I was alone, and I was wrong. He had been there the whole time.

Jesus is not playing a joke on you. He is not a cosmic creeper. He is in every part of your life loving you, guiding you, helping you, watching over you. He said he will never leave us and never forsake us, and he meant it.

You are not alone. He is with you today. When it hurts, when you feel broken, and when you feel abandoned, you are not alone. He is with you. Once again, it has everything to do with who he is.

RESPOND OR RECEIVE?

How do you respond to that kind of love?

You don't.

You receive it. That is the most difficult aspect of knowing Jesus. He isn't impressed by what we offer, but he is moved by what we're willing to receive. Every other religion in the world requires following rules to get a desired result.

HE ISN'T IMPRESSED BY WHAT WE OFFER, BUT HE IS MOVED BY WHAT WE'RE WILLING TO RECIEVE.

Knowing Jesus is about receiving the great news of all he has done for you.

Receiving that kind of love changes you. It not only changes the way you see Jesus; it also changes the way you see yourself and everyone else. Knowing that God walks alongside us through every moment of our life gives us a confidence and a peace that is unshakable. We treat people differently when we receive God's love in our lives. If he won't give up on us, why would we give up on anyone else?

Grace is God blessing us with things we don't deserve. A part of us can't stand grace. Why? Because it has so little to do with us.

Something in us likes to earn what we receive. It makes us uncomfortable to think we are given something of value that we do not deserve.

One day as I was about to check out at the grocery store I noticed a very pretty African American woman standing in front me. Her clothes were impeccable, her hair and makeup spot-on, and she carried herself with a strong confidence. For some reason, I felt I was supposed to give her all the money in my pocket. I only had twenty dollars, but I felt compelled to give it to her. I got scared. What if my offer insulted her? She checked out and headed toward the exit. My heart raced. I felt like I was missing an opportunity to do what I was meant to do. I ran up to her. "Excuse me, ma'am. I really feel like I'm supposed to give you this twenty dollars."

She said, "You feel like you're supposed to give me twenty dollars? Do I look like I need twenty dollars?"

"No ma'am, I'm sorry."

She hurried out the exit and headed to her car. It started pouring rain, and I felt like a complete idiot making the walk of shame to my car. I watched her get into a brand new black S-class Mercedes. Her car came toward me, and as she slowed down to pass, I tapped on her driver's window.

She gave me a look like, "What, idiot?" I apologized and told her I didn't mean to offend her. With the rain pouring into her car, she rested her head on the steering wheel and cried. I had just moved from idiot to jerk.

She said, "I'm sorry, I'm really sorry. My husband just left me, and he emptied all our bank accounts. I do need that twenty dollars. I don't have a dime to my name." Man, tears ensued.

I think we can all relate to how this woman felt when offered something she needed so desperately. Grace does that to us. We need the right attitude or spirit to receive what God has done for us. There are three different spirits with regard to receiving.

The spirit of pride refuses to receive. I have been there so many times—in need of help but unwilling to ask or receive. Pride truly goes before destruction, as we learn in Proverbs 16:18. Pride believes it controls its own destiny, and help is unnecessary. C.S. Lewis describes the mark of hell as being "a ruthless, sleepless, unsmiling concentration upon self."

The spirit of entitlement demands to receive. This attitude says it deserves not only all the blessings that have been given, but even more. Legalistic religion teaches people that it's possible to earn God's favor and grace, which is a man-centered and false idea. Romans 5:8 says, "But God demonstrates his own love for us in this: While we were still sinners, Christ died for us."

We got the most love on the worst day. I'm deeply concerned about people who demand to get what they deserve when God's standard is so much higher than ours. If people actually are demanding to get what they deserve, according to God's standards, they would most certainly not like what they receive.

The spirit of gratitude is thankful to receive. Doesn't that sound so much better? I was preaching in Africa, and afterward a sweet older man walked up, took off his old beat-up watch, and offered it to me. Of course, I refused. I love watches. I have tons of them, and he needed it way more than I did. He didn't speak English very well but said, "If you don't take it, you steal my blessing." More man tears. (This happens more frequently north of forty years old.) Suddenly my pride turned into gratitude. I put it on my wrist, and his face lit up. He paraded me around and showed all the church members my new watch.

Jesus' gift to us is priceless, but so is his heart toward us in giving it. I hope you receive grace gratefully, and I hope it causes you to see Jesus, your-self, and others differently.

EYES ON THE PRIZE

When you live this way, with an awareness that God will always be there for you, something changes in you. Somehow you will want to always be there for him. I'm not talking empty promises or mottos. I mean a deep-down desire to live for Jesus for the rest of your life. Paul talked about it in Hebrews 12:1–3: "Do you see what this means—all these pio-neers who blazed the way, all these veterans cheering us on? It means we'd better get on with it. Strip down, start running—and never quit!

JESUS' GIFT IS PRICELESS, BUT SO IS HIS HEART TOWARD US IN GIVING IT.

No extra spiritual fat, no parasitic sins. Keep your eyes on Jesus, who both began and finished this race we're in" (MSG).

I hate running. I'm convinced running is from the devil. Cycling? That's fine. Wheels were invented because they are far more efficient than legs. Running, in my opinion, is an insult to the creativity and progress of humanity. Even still, this Scripture is amazing. It means heaven is watching us, cheering for us. It's a marathon. We are on a new path with a destination. The destination is Jesus. We need to keep our eyes fixed on him. Whether we are sprinting or jogging or even falling down, the most important thing is that we keep pressing toward Jesus. That is *Jesus Always*. He's always with us. We are always with him. Jesus in everything.

MIGHT AS WELL JUMP

When the disciples found out at the Last Supper that Jesus would be betrayed, they were scared and hurt. The apostle Peter spoke up, making it clear that even if everyone else let Jesus down, he never would. I like Peter because I say dumb things a lot too. Unfortunately, Jesus let Peter know he would deny him three times before morning. And he did.

Before we go judging Peter, let's understand that he became one of the greatest men of God the world has ever known. Peter, when facing crucifixion, demanded to be crucified upside down because he didn't feel worthy to die the same way Jesus did. Peter loved Jesus.

I want to learn from Peter's mistake. Even when we're convinced we would do anything for Jesus, there is always a possibility we might fail. What do you do when you fail? Do you quit? Some people do. You won't. Why? Because you know Jesus is always with you, and you are always with him. Peter knew. In John 6:68, Jesus asked if Peter was going to turn away with all the other disciples who had left. Peter basically said, "Where in the world would I go? You are the Savior." Some people are so afraid of being a hypocrite they never even give Jesus a chance. Jesus knows no matter how earnest we are, there's a hypocrite in all of us. He loves us anyway.

The third and final time Peter denied Jesus, recorded in Luke 22:59–62, is like a scene from a heart-wrenching movie. "About an hour later, someone else spoke up, really adamant: 'He's got to have been with him! He's got "'Galilean"' written all over him.' Peter said, 'Man, I don't know what you're talking about.' At that very moment, the last word hardly off his lips, a rooster crowed. Just then, the Master turned and looked at Peter. Peter remembered what the Master had said to him: 'Before the rooster crows, you will deny me three times.' He went out and cried and cried and cried" (MSG).

That's hard to read. Jesus looks right at him. He is hurt, betrayed, and heartbroken, but he is not done with Peter.

After Jesus was resurrected, the disciples were pretty lost. Peter undoubtedly felt guilty from his epic fail.

A MAN CUT OFF FROM HIS FUTURE WILL ALWAYS GO BACK TO HIS PAST.

"Simon Peter, Thomas (nicknamed 'Twin'), Nathanael from Cana in Galilee, the brothers Zebedee, and two other disciples were together. Simon Peter announced, '*I'm going fishing.' The rest of them replied, 'We're going with you'*" (John 21:1–3 MSG, emphasis mine).

A man cut off from his future will always go back to his past.

Notice how easy it was for all the disciples to jump right back into the life they lived before they knew Jesus. Isn't it funny how many people jump on board when you are in a poor state of mind?

"They went out and got into the boat. They caught nothing that night" (John 21:3, MSG). Don't even look back. There is nothing there. Looking back opens up the possibility of going back.

"But when the sun came up, Jesus was standing on the beach, *but they didn't recognize him*" (John 21:4, MSG, emphasis mine). When you go back to your past, it's hard to see Jesus for who he really is. Our vision becomes unclear.

"Jesus spoke to them: 'Good morning! Did you catch anything for breakfast?' They answered, 'No.' He said, 'Throw the net off the right side of the boat and see what happens.' They did what he said. All of a sudden there were so many fish in it, they weren't strong enough to pull it in" (John 21:5-6, MSG). Jesus didn't tell them something they hadn't already tried. They were professional fisherman. They knew every trick in the book. You may try everything within your power to make things work your own way. He was essentially saying, *Don't just do something; do something because I told you to.*

It was a record-breaking catch!

"Then the disciple Jesus loved said to Peter, 'It's the Master'" (John 21:7, MSG). John didn't just suddenly recognize Jesus' face from far away. John knew it was Jesus because of the fish. When Jesus is in your life, incredible things happen all around you. I love this next part so much.

"When Simon Peter realized that it was the Master, he threw on some clothes, for he was stripped for work, and dove into the sea" (John 21:7, MSG). Peter had already denied Jesus. He wasn't about to do that again. He may not have recognized him first, but he was determined to reach him first. He wasn't about to play it cool—he goes Michael Phelps on everybody. The other disciples had to bring in the fish they caught. Peter didn't care. He saw his shot at redemption and took it.

This wasn't the first time Jesus had caused a miraculous catch of fish in Peter's life. It happened when they first met. In that particular moment, Peter became so aware of Jesus' goodness and his own sin that he begged Jesus to leave because he felt unworthy. His feeling of unworthiness and his own desire to live a better life caused him to have a desire to *create distance from Jesus.* Oh my, how different this other story is.

Peter was not as alone as he felt. Jesus came and found Peter. He won't give up on us either. This time Peter fully understands his own unworthiness and the goodness of Jesus, and he jumps into the water to close the distance between him and Jesus as soon as possible. He was saying, "I know I'm a mess. The only way to fix it is Jesus. I have to get to Jesus."

"The other disciples followed in the boat, towing the net full of fish, for they were not far from shore, about a hundred yards. When they landed, they saw a fire of burning coals there, with fish on it, and some bread" (John 21:8-9). Why are we told that Jesus was on shore cooking on coals? The coals are no coincidence. The last place Peter denied Jesus was by coals of fire. Jesus will restore you at the very place you deny him. The coals of our con-

JESUS WILL RESTORE YOU AT THE VERY PLACE YOU DENY HIM.

science burn hot when we fail God, but his love for us burns even hotter. That's redemption.

"Jesus said to them, 'Bring some of the fish you have just caught.' So Simon Peter climbed back into the boat and dragged the net ashore. It was full of large fish—153 to be exact—but even with so many, the net was not torn. Jesus said to them, 'Come and have breakfast.' None of the disciples dared ask him, 'Who are you?' They knew it was the Lord. Jesus came, took the bread and gave it to them, and did the same with the fish" (John 21:10-13). Breakfast? With Jesus? Jesus ain't mad at ya. We need the reassurance that Jesus brings. To think that Jesus would share breakfast with Peter after his failure says much about who Jesus is. When people betray me, I want to unfriend them, block them, and sometimes slap them. Jesus invites us close. He serves us in our weakness.

If you finish the story, Jesus goes on to ask three times if Peter loves him (John 21:15-17). Peter says yes the first two times, and the third time he is almost hurt. He says, "Lord, You know all things, surely you know I love you." Jesus tells him, "Shepherd my sheep"—basically, "if you love me, then live for me by doing the things I have taught you." Jesus wanted Peter to know that what was in front of him was greater than what was behind him.

Jesus Always means Jesus is always with us, and we are always with him, even in the face of failure. You won't quit. You will fail, but never quit loving him and serving him. You get up when you are weak, tired, broken, and keep your eyes fixed on Jesus. Why? There is a longing in all of us for permanence, and it was put there by God. The only way it can be fulfilled is by recognizing that life must become Jesus always, in everything. *Jesus Always.*

THE LOVE I'M

TALKING ABOUT IS

THE KIND OF LOVE

THAT YOU REALIZE IS

A FURIOUS, DYNAMIC,

FAR-REACHING LOVE.

CHAPTER FIVE:
the surrender

"The thief comes only to steal and kill and destroy; I have come that they may have life, and have it to the full. I am the good shepherd. The good shepherd lays down his life for the sheep . . . No one takes it from me, but I lay it down of my own accord. I have authority to lay it down and authority to take it up again."

— **John 10:10-11, 18**

BOARD GAMES GALORE

Let's talk about board games. I've loved board games since I was a kid. Twister is not a board game. I don't care if it has a board. Any game requiring flexibility does not qualify as a board game. Battleship? Board game. Stratego? Board game. Sorry? Board game. Operation? Ah, skill game. It says so on the box. Plus, it has electronics, which disqualifies it in general . . . not to mention it has a picture of a naked guy with a really bad haircut. Dominoes is not really a board game, but, oh man, I used to love it.

Monopoly is a classic—super fun to play—but it takes forever for anybody to win. I love that, but it seems no one ever wants to finish the game. You ever notice that? Why? Because people have divorced and ended friendships over this game. It seems like it always ends with something like someone accusing their sweet elderly aunt of stealing orange 500 dollar bills from the bank. (I'm simply relaying the story of a friend.)

One of the games I loved when I was a kid was Clue. I don't know if that's a seventies thing or whatever, but Clue is just amazing. I don't think anyone my age would be able to spell the word *colonel* without playing Clue. I learned what a conservatory was from playing Clue. I had no idea. It's kind of a little greenhouse sort of room. I learned that even though you are successful and smart enough to build a massive mansion, you can be so dumb that you forget to build a bathroom. That's something they need to work on in the game right there. Colonel Mustard with a wrench in the bathroom—that should happen at some point. I also learned that you can hate someone so much that you can actually murder them with a candlestick. Even though a revolver was a viable option, you still chose a candlestick to kill this person.

Another one of my favorite games as a kid was Checkers. You just go diagonal—you're jumping things, saying, "King me!" Then I got a little bit older and started liking Chess, and what I love about Chess is the strategy. One of the principles of Chess, if you don't know much about it, is the development of your pieces. You want to strategically situate all your pieces in order to control the center of the board as soon as possible while maintaining a solid pawn structure.

Those people sacrificing pawns all over the place may gain an advantage early. But once you get to the mid-game and the end-game, they're vulnerable to attacks from their opponent if their pawn structure is weak. Ultimately, the goal is to put your opponent's king in checkmate while keeping your own safe and defended. When the

THE DEVIL IS REAL, BUT HE ISN'T EQUAL TO GOD.

king is being attacked, but has an option to move, it is called, "Check." Checkmate means you are attacking the other person's king, and they have no viable move. You've trapped the king, and the game is over. Now, if you see that you are going to lose, and a loss is imminent, there is a move in Chess called Surrender or Resign. You tip over your king, which simply means that, although you're not in checkmate right now, you can see how this is playing out. You surrender. The game is over. You lose.

UNWORTHY OPPONENT?

In art, balance and contrast

are crucial. Whether something is symmetrical or asymmetrical, there still needs to be some balance of distribution to keep us from feeling unsettled. The same is true with contrast. Contrast is the difference in two related elements such as color, shape, type, texture, alignment, or movement. The greater the contrast, the more a viewer's attention is obtained.

Literature and film usually possess a strong sense of contrast, especially when dealing with good and evil. People try to create a sense of balance and contrast with characters. If there is a great hero, tension is created with an equally powerful, yet evil, villain. Harry Potter has Voldemort. Superman has Lex Luthor. Maximus has Commodus. Austin Powers has Dr. Evil.

Many people think of God and the devil in this same way, but it is simply not true. Without creating some deep discussion, Satan is a created being who was banished from heaven and awaits his unavoidable punishment from God. He is no more equal to God than the weight of a feather is to the collective mass of the universe. The devil and all fallen angels exist primarily to confuse and destroy the relationship between the Father and his children.

The devil is real, but he isn't equal to God.

Even though we know these are uneven opponents, in classic Ingmar Bergman style, let's imagine that God and the devil were engaged in a cosmic Chess match. With each move, the devil has been trying to destroy everything God has ever done. And sometimes, it even looks like he's winning—maybe even calling out, "Check!"

I'm sure the devil thought he was going to win when Adam and Eve disobeyed God and took that fruit. They had to face the consequences of their actions and nothing was ever the same again. The two had to leave their home, and walk away from all they'd ever known. They couldn't enjoy God living among them, walking with them, talking with them face-to-face. It looked like a win for the devil. But God stitched together clothes for them—to cover them from the elements of the weather, but also to cover their guilt and shame and provide another way for hope to win. I'm sure the devil thought he was going to win when the children of Israel were trapped at the banks of the Red Sea. Fleeing for their lives from slavery in Egypt, they hit a dead end. As Pharaoh's armies approached closer and closer, God made his move and split the sea down the middle, providing a miraculous escape route for the Israelites. The devil didn't win.

I'm sure the devil thought he was going to win as Esther learned that King Xerxes inadvertently signed a decree, calling for the eradication of the Jewish people. Haman had tricked the Persian king into legalizing a BC Holocaust. But God used Esther to save an entire race of people, preventing genocide during a time in which her people had been oppressed, beaten, and displaced by the ruling empires. The devil didn't win.

Then Jesus was born, and I'm sure the devil thought he was going to win when Herod found out that the Messiah had been born. The evil king had all of the males two years old and younger slaughtered, but Jesus' family escaped, seeking refuge in Egypt until Herod's death. The devil didn't win.

It looked like an easy win after Jesus had fasted in the wilderness for forty days. He was hungry, thirsty, tired, and vulnerable. If there was ever a time the devil could make his move, it was then. He pulled out all the stops. He offered food, power, authority, and all the kingdoms of the earth. But Jesus didn't waver, and the devil didn't win.

I'm sure the devil thought he was going to win when Jesus came out of that wilderness, full of authority and power given by *God*, not the devil. Jesus opened the scroll of Isaiah in the synagogue and declared to everyone around him that the Scriptures referred to him and that he was, in fact, the Messiah. All the religious leaders attacked him, driving him to the edge of a cliff with intentions of pushing him to his death. But he moved through their midst as easily as the Israelites crossed the Red Sea on dry land, and the devil didn't win.

THE SURRENDER

We could talk about that cosmic Chess match for an entire book. There have been many times that the Enemy thought he would win, but I want to focus on one pivotal moment.

For the devil, it seemed the ultimate checkmate was the cross. Jesus had been whipped, beaten, tortured, and left to hang on two beams of wood until he died. We all know Jesus had the power to avoid this. He healed people all the time. He raised people from the dead. He calmed the wind and the waves, and he drove out demons. If he could save anyone from death, surely he could save himself! But in that moment, instead of fighting, instead of calling on all the authority and power he possessed, Jesus did the unthinkable.

The King resigned. The Surrender.

This surrender of Jesus is either the ultimate no-win situation where he realized he had no more options—he *must* surrender—or it's a different kind of surrender. It's something else. In John 10:11, Jesus says, "I am the good shepherd. The good shepherd lays down his life for the sheep."

Lays down his life.

Why does the good shepherd lay down his life for his sheep? The answer is pretty simple. The good shepherd loves his sheep more than he loves himself. Before his own death, Jesus said to his disciples in John 15:13, "Greater love has no one than this: to lay down one's life for one's friends."

Then he laid down his life for his friends.

Think about that. *Laying down your life for your friends.* I don't want you to think of God's love for you in the way we throw love around. "I love that movie. I love my wife. I love ice cream. I love football." The word *love* can become so tired, and we trivialize it. The love I'm talking about is the kind of love that you realize is a furious, dynamic, far-reaching love that came through galaxies and time and space itself to rescue you!

Stakes beyond our imagination!

The stakes Jesus had to face were beyond our imagination. The creator of the universe, the supreme king, paying the ultimate price. In the Old Testament, in order to be forgiven, people didn't have the luxury we have of saying, "Jesus, forgive me. God, forgive me." In ancient Jewish culture, on the Day of Atonement the high priest would take two goats. He would slaughter one goat and sprinkle the blood of that goat upon the Holy of Holies, the innermost part of the temple, to make atonement and restitution for all the sins of the people and himself. It's the only time of year that the priests would enter.

He would put all of the sins of the people upon the other goat, known as the scapegoat. Imagine going to church and the preacher saying, "God we take all of our sin, and we put it on this goat. Everything we have done, we put the responsibility and the blame on this goat." Then he would banish that goat to the wilderness outside the camp forever. The camp and the place of God represented the favor and blessing of God. To be outside and banished in the wilderness meant you never gained access again to the favor of God.

Our King became these goats. He was slaughtered. We all know that, but he was also banished. He had to be forsaken and banished by his father. The cross was the full measure of God's anger and wrath toward humanity, in order that we could be saved. All of the sin that we have in our life? God simply will not permit it. God doesn't wink at sin the way we do. He doesn't say, "Oh, boys will be boys" or "Girls will be girls." That's not the way God is. God hates sin. God gave Jesus judgment with no grace on that cross. Why did he have to be forsaken?

So we could be accepted.

In order that we could be free, Jesus, the ultimate king, had to pay the price. Not only did he die, but there also had to be a moment on the cross when the sky went dark and God himself, the Father, turned his back on his own son. The reason Jesus cried out, "Father, why have you forsaken me?" wasn't because he felt forsaken. He *was* forsaken. God had to abandon his own son. That's what I mean by stakes we can't imagine.

GAME CHANGER

The devil looked at Jesus on the cross. The sky had gone dark on Jesus' lifeless body. He wanted to wait for the right moment because he'd been foiled so many times before.

He didn't want to celebrate prematurely. He felt pretty confident at this point. He looked up at the cross and believed he had won. He got a sick smile on his face.

Have you been at a point in your life where you feel like all your hope was lost? Like the Enemy was staring right in your face ready to celebrate the end of your hope? Have you ever felt finished?

Right before he died, Jesus declared, "It is finished." *Tetelestai.* The Greek word is an accounting term. When you paid off an item, they gave you a receipt bearing this word that means "paid in full." Jesus is saying, "There is nothing left for me to accomplish. I have fulfilled everything. God, you turned your back on me. Your wrath was against me. I made it through that. I have done everything in this life. Now all there is for me to do is bow my head and give up my spirit." He said, "Tetelestai." It is finished. *It* is finished means *we* are never finished.

Jesus' life was not taken from him. In this game, the ultimate king has the power not only to surrender his life but to take it up again. John 10:17–18 says, "The reason my Father loves me is that I lay down my life—only to take it up again. No one takes it from me, but I lay it down of my own accord. I have authority to lay it down and authority to take it up again. This command I received from my Father." Jesus surrenders and lays it all down and pays the price so we don't have to be banished. We don't have to die. The ultimate king did both for us.

Do you see what Jesus is doing with the Surrender? He's changing the game. For you. For me. Forever. When you think it's over, it's not over. Jesus *changed the game*. When you find out that news that seems so heartbreaking—"I'm sorry to tell you, you have cancer"—what happens? The devil wants to inch in your face and grin ear to ear and say, "I win."

It's not over.

When you commit the same sin over and over, and you think you can't stop doing it. When you do it one more time, the devil likes to get right up next to you and whisper in your ear, "I win."

It's not over.

When there's something in your life that you can't distance yourself from. No matter how far you run or where you go, that old thing follows you. The thing that you did so long ago, and you can never lose sight of it. The devil says, "I win."

It's not over.

They laid him in the grave. They put a massive rock in front of the opening and sealed it. They put guards in front of the grave to make sure that Jesus didn't get out, that no one took him out. Friday goes by, and the devil says, "Whew." All of Saturday goes by, but he doesn't want to say anything prematurely. The early hours of Sunday come. This time, he's not going to whisper. This time, he's going to shout it with everything he has. Because he is certain that there are no more options. He looks at that grave and says, "Jesus! I WIN!"

It's not over.

Why? Because Jesus changed the game. As a mat-

TIME IS NOT LINEAR WITH GOD AS IT IS WITH US. JESUS WON BEFORE THERE WAS EVEN A BATTLE.

ter of fact, the devil is mistaken. He was never in the game to begin with. Revelation 13 talks about Jesus having died for us before the world even began. Don't be confused. Time is not linear with God as it is with us. Jesus won before there was even a battle. The outcome was predetermined. The devil never had a chance—with your destiny or against Jesus.

Never give up. Never give up on yourself or your family or those who have left the faith. Never give up on your future when it looks like it's falling apart. Never give up on your destiny when you feel like it's over. That stone exploded out of the way. An earthquake. That grave couldn't keep Jesus down. He saved his best move for last. He came to life by his own power. Conquered death forevermore. We never have to worry about death. We have eternal life, and he foiled the devil once again.

The devil will never win this game because Jesus has already won. He's alive today! Jesus is alive. We have hope because of him and only because of him.

This isn't a cosmic Chess match. It's a cosmic obliteration. Hope over hate, love over fear, life over death, and Jesus over it all.

It is finished. *It is finished* means we are never finished.

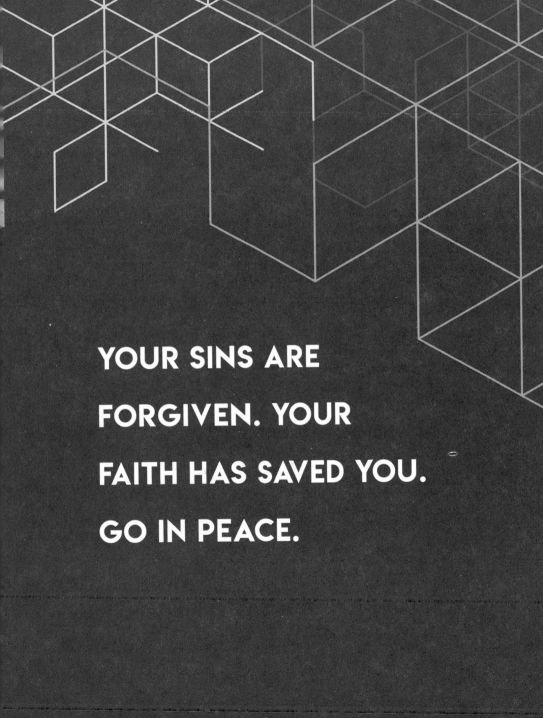

YOUR SINS ARE
FORGIVEN. YOUR
FAITH HAS SAVED YOU.
GO IN PEACE.

INTERLUDE
the vessel

She closes the door to the small room at the inn and crumples to the floor like a wounded child. At first her face is expressionless, then her chin quivers, and she breaks. Tears pour down her face, and her thick makeup runs. She takes off her bracelets and earrings and lays them on the floor beside her.

Once she was breathtaking, but years of hard living have etched themselves above her brow and turned her once-shimmering eyes sad. Living in constant fear and sometimes terrible abuse has made her a survivor. No one has ever taken care of her, and in this moment, she feels it.

The music outside her window is loud, as usual. This part of town is known for late-night rendezvous and places to get in trouble. This lifestyle has kept her alive for the last twelve years.

She releases her fist and looks at the money in her hand. A single denarius, almost enough to pay for five more days' rent. The man who just left had promised her so much more, so many times. As a professional she has trained herself to ignore anything personal, yet his talk of love, commitment, and family still sounded comforting, even sweet. She wishes she hadn't even listened to him. Again.

With a deep breath, she wipes away the last of her tears, collects her things, and makes her way to a small table beside the bed, the only furniture in the room. She opens a wooden box on the table and looks at the money inside. Tonight's earnings make it a total of fifteen denarii. She closes the box. Beside it rests a beautifully crafted bottle of alabaster. Removing the lid, she lifts the empty bottle to her nose, breathing in the sweet fragrance. She sticks her finger just inside the top, then rubs either side of her neck.

Exhaustion settles over her from a grueling evening. Yet the night is not over. She straightens her hair and moistens her lips. Hearing the knock at the door, she wipes her eyes quickly, trying to get herself together. With a deep breath, she opens the door, and her eyes light up like she's the happiest girl in the world. At least that's what it looks like to him.

Morning comes sooner than expected. The sunlight pouring in the window takes her back to when she was a little girl on her uncle's farm, before he started treating her the wrong way. She loved sleeping in the stables near all the little lambs. How innocent they were. How innocent she was. She feels guilty for even entertaining such thoughts. Time to get up. There are things to be done.

She knocks on a door downstairs. The old man who answers the door immediately asks her about the rent. She hands him two denarii. He's not impressed. "One more week," he mumbles. "Don't ever pay me late again."

The marketplace is alive at this time of day. People from all over sell their merchandise and try to hustle anyone and everyone. She peruses the sea of commerce, carrying the beautiful bottle with her. Stopping at a souk, she picks up a red dress.

"It look beautiful on you," says the teenage boy selling it.

She smiles. "How much?"

"Six denarii. It from Egypt. Silk. It beautiful. It soft. You buy. Six denarii."
She reaches in her pocket and pulls out three denarii, hands it to him, then leans down to his level. "I buy. Three denarii. You take."

He looks a little embarrassed as if he'd been caught doing something wrong. He whispers, "OK," and then smiles.

She walks up to a merchant table with dozens of beautiful bottles similar to the one she is holding. Some empty, some full of oil, ointments, or perfumes. The man in charge greets her with a kiss on her cheek. "You have come back."

"Yes, I ran out."

"Well, what do want this time?"

"The same thing. It smells like heaven."

"Well, I don't have any more of what you bought last time."

Disappointment fills her eyes.

"I know. I am sorry, but I do have something from the Himalayas. From a queen. It is called Nard. Special spices even I don't know how to identify. Here." He hands her a small cloth.

Her eyes light up as she smells it. "How much?"

"It is expensive. But then again, you have expensive taste. Three hundred denarii."

She looks devastated. "Three hundred? I have only ten."

"There are other things you may like."

"I want this one."

"Well, give me the ten you have, and maybe we can work something out for the rest." He raises an eyebrow; his smile turns devilish.

For a split second her eyes flash with pain, but she musters up her charm. "We have a deal."

He takes a black flask and pours the precious perfume into her jar.
"This is a beautiful bottle. Pure alabaster?"

"It was a gift, from my aunt when I was a child."

"Very beautiful, just like you."

She forces one more smile as she thanks him.

"You know where I live." he says. "Monday nights will be fine."

*Walking back to her room she wonders how this weekly commitment
will affect her regular clientele. It will just have to work.*

*A few weeks later, she hears someone talking outside her window in
the street below. She sees a man being followed by a large crowd.
What is he selling to get so many followers? Though she strains to
hear, he is simply too far away. She decides to go find out what all
the fuss is about.*

*Down on the street she senses a difference in the atmosphere of the
marketplace. Everyone is listening. Hundreds of people, just listening
"Who is he?" she whispers to herself, rudely pressing through the*

bodies to get closer. She finally sees him—a young man to have such a large audience.

He is in the middle of a thought. "You're blessed when you've lost it all. God's kingdom is there for the finding. You're blessed when the tears flow freely. Joy comes with the morning." His piercing eyes look right at her when he says it. It's the first time she can remember a man looking at her with such kindness. Nothing has ever jolted her the way these beautiful words just have. He moves through the market as he talks, and the crowd follows, passing her by. She stands, eyes closed, pondering what she has just heard. Joy comes in the morning? How could this be possible? Regret and shame have been her constant waking thoughts. Despite what experience has taught her, something in her heart believes the man.

Ignoring several knocks on her door throughout the evening, she angers regular customers with missed appointments. But sleep eludes her. Thousands of thoughts run through her head. She smiles as her thoughts drift to her favorite little lamb on her uncle's farm. The love in that man's eyes reminded her of that little lamb.

By now she's heard the rumors. His name is Jesus. Some say he is the Messiah, that he's done great miracles. Some say he's just another *fraud. She's never been very religious, but she cannot deny the fact that something in her has changed just from seeing him. Hearing his voice. Feeling the pure love in his eyes. They say he'll be having dinner at a local Pharisee's house tomorrow night. She develops a plan.*

The next day she wakes up with a feeling she can't describe. Crawling out of bed, she smiles at the empty room. "I have nothing to my name, yet I am happy." Her smile turns to laughter as she readies herself for the day ahead.

That evening she approaches the house where Jesus is supposed to be. Her thoughts have turned from hopeful to hesitant. She has worn her best dress and labored in preparing. "What if he wasn't even looking at me? What if I just heard what I wanted to?" Despite her thoughts, she presses on to the place where Jesus is, catching a glimpse of him with all of the religious leaders. Does he know some of these men are not as holy as they appear?

No more time for contemplation. She takes the alabaster bottle in her hand and inhales deeply. She walks into the room. Every eye is fixed on her. Conversations die. It doesn't matter. His eyes are so pure. Kneeling in front of him, she pours her life savings on his feet, unaware of the gasps of horror in the room. Her tears mingle with the

precious perfume as she wipes his feet. She thinks to herself, Thank
you, thank you for loving me. You were right. Joy came this morning

One of the religious men observes who she is, and Jesus corrects him,
but she doesn't notice. She is caught up in this moment. Every failure,
every hurt, every shameful thing she has ever done and every painful
word that was ever spoken to her—all of it flowed from her heart.
Jesus looks at her and says, "Your sins are forgiven. Your faith has
saved you. Go in peace."

Everyone in town will hear about what happened tonight. She will
lose her business. She will lose everything. But none of that matters.
Her debts do not matter. Her past does not matter. All that matters is
what Jesus just said to her. "Your sins are forgiven."

WE WANT FREEDOM.
WE WANT LOVE.
WE WANT JOY,
PERFECTION,
PEACE,
WHOLENESS,
PURPOSE.

CHAPTER SIX:
paradise

"One of the criminals who hung there hurled insults at him: 'Aren't you the Messiah? Save yourself and us!' But the other criminal rebuked him. 'Don't you fear God,' he said, 'since you are under the same sentence? We are punished justly, for we are getting what our deeds deserve. But this man has done nothing wrong.' Then he said, 'Jesus, remember me when you come into your kingdom.' Jesus answered him, 'Truly I tell you, today you will be with me in paradise.'"

— Luke 23:39–43

IN PARADISE

I went to Hawaii a few years ago and finally learned what all the fuss is about. I've seen pictures, of course. I watched *Magnum P.I.* and *Hawaii Five-0*, but nothing compares to actually being there. The deepest blue water and black, monolithic volcanoes are the backdrop for dark green jungles and forests where colors look like they dripped off the brush of a brilliant artist. In addition to all its beauty, there is a peaceful vibe. When you factor in a local dish called Loco Moco, it's pretty transcendent. Now, when I hear the word *paradise*, Hawaii is the image that first comes to my mind.

If you search for #paradise on Twitter, you'll find that most of the top posts contain pictures of beautiful landscapes, clear waters and beaches, or whimsical looking forests. They all contain the common elements of beauty, serenity, and peace. It's what we crave. We want peace, *shalom*. We long for beautiful scenery where we can enjoy life without stress or worry. We want to be inspired by nature and feel the warmth of the sun on our skin without getting a sunburn. We want freedom. We want love. We want joy, perfection, peace, wholeness, purpose.

We all have our ideas of what paradise on earth is like. But what's paradise like after we die?

THE CRIMINAL ON THE CROSS

Early Friday morning, he was exhausted. He had been kept awake all night, arrested the night before. They made the journey to the first official's home where they conducted an illegal pre-trial to get as much dirt on him as they could. On the way to the next official's house, he knew the lies and false accusations that lay before him, yet he walked on. This official went over his track record to find *the* crime he had committed that would put him in his place. When they couldn't find anything, they decided to lie. They had already paid off one guy to frame him. Next was a trial in the highest religious court. Without any real evidence, he was tried for blasphemy. They looked for false witnesses and found two with contradicting stories. Though he was found guilty, this court had no authority to have him executed, so he was transferred to a Roman official.

After reviewing the case, the new official knew right off the bat that this was foul play. But instead of doing anything about it, he transferred the case to another district. After all, he *did* have his constituents to please, and the man *had* been a bit of a trouble maker.

So they took the convict to the new district, where they beat and laughed at him more and then sent him back to the previous district. And this time, the official's constituents wanted blood, so he gave it to them. He had the man beaten, whipped, chained, and ultimately, sent out of town carrying his future—a cross—on his back. As the man stumbled his way to Golgotha, a huge crowd gathered to watch the spectacle. They laughed, spat, and threw rotten food at the man journeying to his own grave. And when he finally got there, they drove the nails through his hands and ankles. He cried out in agony as they raised the cross between two other men already hanging and waited for him to die the slowest, most painful death the Romans had ever invented.

Nailed to the beams in a way that would cause a person's lungs to collapse if he or she simply hung there, those who were crucified ultimately suffocated to death. They would push down into their nailed feet and pull up into their pierced hands in feeble attempts to lift their bodies and gasp for air. Of course, the pain was intolerable. They'd collapse again. They'd repeat that cycle until their bodies couldn't take anymore. They'd give up the fight, allowing their lungs to compress, releasing their last breath.

In his final few precious moments of life, the man on Jesus' left began to laugh. His laughter turned to mocking insults. "If you're really the King of the Jews, why don't you get down and save yourself? Oh, and by the way, save me too!"

The man on Jesus' right was the logical one. "You're hanging on a cross too," he said to the laughing man. "You really can't talk right now. You at least deserve your sentence. This guy did nothing wrong!" And at that moment, he looked into Jesus' eyes with the last bit of hope a man could muster before his dying breath, and said, "Jesus, remember me." That was his only hope. Remember me.

Jesus pushed down on his feet and pulled up on his hands, took in as much air as he could, and said, "Truly, you'll be with me today in paradise."

Paradise. What is paradise? The word he used is the ancient Persian word *paradeisos* which means enclosure, garden, or park. As beautiful as Hawaii is, I don't think that thief on the cross died and woke up with Jesus on the island of Maui, wearing a lei, and listening to Don Ho. What is this paradise to which Jesus was referring?

Where did that guy on the cross wake up after he

took his last breath?

CHERUBS AND CHOCOLATE

Some people give very little thought to what happens after this life. I once did a sermon series on heaven, and we took a film crew out to a rowdy area of town on a Friday night to get some ideas of what people think. Drunk people and spiritual conversations are a pretty entertaining combination.

You might be shocked at how many people think heaven consists of clouds and naked babies playing harps. I'm not sure, maybe the stork guy invented that one too. A lot of people believe in heaven; there are just very different views on what it looks like.

I asked one lady to describe what heaven will be like. Her answer was short, candid, and though it is not in the Bible, I wish it was. She said, "Chocolate." I can picture it now. Her idea of heaven sounds like Willy Wonka's factory. And we all know how that went. (Call me old school, but Gene Wilder was the best.) Other responses included, "Just, like, a lot of people, just people chilling, no arguing and stuff, more like a never-ending party." "We turn into angels." "Flying around, wherever you want."

Heaven, for most people, is probably their own idea of Utopia. Someone said, "Take the one thing you love the most, and you do it forever." Uh, really? Please think about that for a minute. Forever? That would probably be closer to the definition of hell, no matter how much you love something. Remember Tom Hanks in *Castaway*? He had his own private paradise, but he didn't seem to have too much fun. Thank God for Wilson, though.

MY PRIVILEGE

As a pastor, I have the privilege of celebrating life's highs and lows with people. I share the joy of monumental moments, the best of the best! But I also see the worst of the worst. I mourn with those who experience loss and tragedy in their lives. I sit at some of my favorite people's death beds, say goodbye to them, and perform their funerals.

We can make jokes all day long regarding drunk people's ideas about heaven, but sometimes it turns into a more serious conversation. What really happened to my friend Dave, the friend we lost too soon? How do we talk about heaven in the midst of losing a child, spouse, or par-

BEING WITH JESUS IS PARADISE. THERE WILL BE NO SADNESS, SICKNESS, OR SORROW IN HEAVEN.

ent when it feels like hell on earth? Where is she? Is he okay? Will I ever get to see my loved one again? These are questions anyone would have in these desperate moments.

I could try to describe how beautiful heaven might be, like the elvish land of Rivendell from *Lord of the Rings* or something. In fact, Revelation gives a description of heaven with beautiful imagery that's supposed to evoke even better feelings than if you were imagining Hawaii. But the truth is, even though there are beautiful descriptions in the Bible, I think we miss something really important Jesus said to this poor, wretched thief on the cross. He said, "Truly I tell you, today you will be *with me* in paradise.

Being with Jesus is paradise. There will be no sadness, sickness, or sorrow in heaven, but remember, Jesus is The Supreme Answer for Life who settled in our 'hood. He's the one who loves us more than anyone. We're his favorite. He gave everything for us. He personifies hope, life, and creativity. He is peace. We know that Jesus is the Alpha and Omega. He started it all, and he finishes it all.

This means Jesus Always.

With sincerest apologies to my friends in the Aloha state, *being with Jesus* is paradise.

PARADISE LOST

In the beginning, when God created the earth, it was paradise. Full of lush gardens, streams, and all sorts of fruit and animals, it was warm and peaceful, with only the sounds of nature to fill Adam and Eve's ears. They lived in unbroken harmony as God walked among them in the garden. They lived in perfect community, eating freely from the Tree of Life, nothing to disrupt the paradise created for them. But we look around today, and that's just not the case anymore. Broken relationships, divided territories, a sick planet, broken people. Peace isn't something we experience. Watch just five minutes of any news station or scroll down your newsfeed on Facebook, and you'll see that something has gone wrong in the world. Genocide, racism, oppression, greed, selfishness, and a lack of responsibility run rampant. History is plagued with the abuse of power, people, and the earth's resources. It's not only in large catastrophic events where we sense brokenness; we also see it in our own relationships, thoughts, and habits. Our proclivity toward sin is so inherent that we're left pondering the age-

OUR PROCLIVITY TOWARD SIN IS SO INHERENT THAT WE'RE LEFT PONDERING THE AGE-OLD QUESTION, "HOW DID WE FALL SO FAR?"

old question, "How did we fall so far?"

And how can we get back to the way it's supposed to be?

PARADISE FOUND

When we die, something happens. Our souls leave our bodies. Christians believe that in that moment we are with Jesus in paradise, the resting place. We're with the one who created it all, the Alpha, where we experience pure love and joy and peace.

But did you know it gets even better?

Jesus talked about being in paradise with him immediately after we die, but he also talked about the final day. We've discussed how Jesus is Alpha, the creator, the beginning of it all. But what about that Omega part? The end? Jesus isn't just at the end of our own individual lives. He's bigger than that.

Jesus is the Omega of it all. Just as he was in the beginning, he will be in the end. The *very* end. When Jesus returns to earth to fix it all. To return to paradise.

The day Jesus returns, those who have passed will come back to life. No, not like *The Walking Dead* (I miss

Hershel). Way less creepy. Those who knew Jesus will come alive once again. Literally. We will be given new (and hopefully improved) bodies. We'll walk around, run, hug our friends and family members. We'll get to work for God, create, and learn. We'll get to eat good food and laugh and listen to great music and watch football. I wonder if there's a Super Bowl at the resurrection. What a ridiculous question. Of course there will be a Super Bowl, and Dallas will beat the Patriots every year.

And at the end, at the resurrection, when it's all said and done, this is what Scripture has to say:

> Then I saw "a new heaven and a new earth," for the first heaven and the first earth had passed away, and there was no longer any sea. I saw the Holy City, the new Jerusalem, coming down out of heaven from God, prepared as a bride beautifully dressed for her husband. And I heard a loud voice from the throne saying, "Look! God's dwelling place is now among the people, and he will dwell with them. They will be

his people, and God himself will be with them and be their God. 'He will wipe every tear from their eyes. There will be no more death' Or mourning or crying or pain, for the old order of things has passed away."

He who was seated on the throne said, "I am making everything new!" Then he said, "Write this down, for these words are trustworthy and true."

He said to me: "It is done. I am the Alpha and the Omega, the Beginning and the End. To the thirsty I will give water without cost from the spring of the water of life. Those who are victorious will inherit all this, and I will be their God and they will be my children." (Revelation 21:1–7)

Jesus is seated on that throne, promising that in the end, death dies, life lives, and God walks among us again. A physical, tangible rebirth and renewal of the earth will come, and all things will be made new. In the end, it will

A PHYSICAL, TANGIBLE REBIRTH AND RENEWAL OF THE EARTH WILL COME, AND ALL THINGS WILL BE MADE NEW.

be as it was in the beginning. All of creation will be brought back together as a paradise.

This is the hope we hold on to. This is the reality in which we live, where Jesus is Alpha and Omega, first and always. It's the hope we cling to in the midst of tragedy and despair. It's the truth we proclaim on Easter and every day as the people of God. This is the truth that gives us the strength and audacity to taunt death. "Death has been swallowed up in victory. Where, O death, is your victory? Where, O death, is your sting?" (1 Corinthians 15:55).

Sometimes death and loss seem to be too much.

Death is a big enemy because it seems so final. In this world, in this life, it is. But not with Jesus. If you can't believe that, then right now you're living a life that may say Jesus First, but *believes* Death Wins. And that's just a flat-out lie.

Jesus *precedes* us. He is the Alpha. Jesus was before life, and Jesus was before creation. Jesus *outlasts* us. We live eternally, but he is already there. His majesty and mystery will be unfolding continually in the ages to come. Jesus will be after the new creation. He is the Omega. He is the one at the end point. All of history and eternity is rushing toward him. Will you?

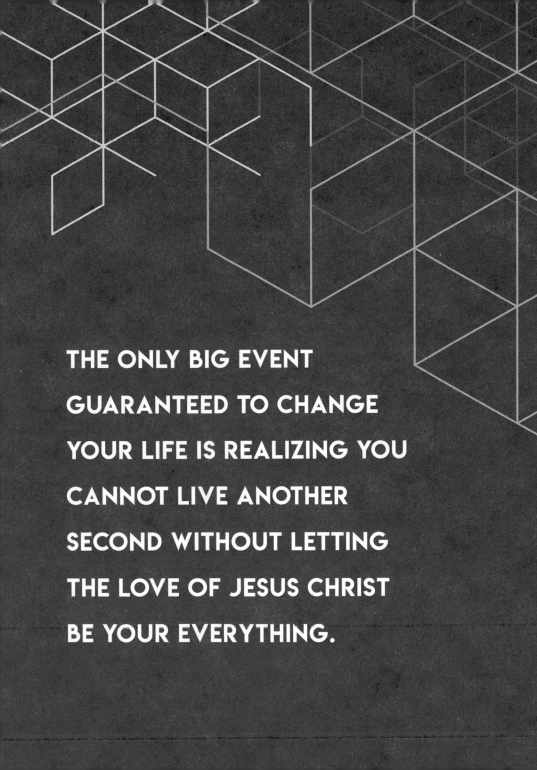

THE ONLY BIG EVENT
GUARANTEED TO CHANGE
YOUR LIFE IS REALIZING YOU
CANNOT LIVE ANOTHER
SECOND WITHOUT LETTING
THE LOVE OF JESUS CHRIST
BE YOUR EVERYTHING.

CHAPTER SEVEN:
the big event

DREAMS

When I was a kid I loved Michael McDonald. If you don't know the song "I Keep Forgettin'," I will pray for you until you hear it. I'll even give you a free pass if you only know it from the sample used in Warren G's "Regulate." I grew up listening to Stevie Wonder, Donny Hathaway, and Michael Jackson. Michael McDonald was a soulful white dude and, as a singer myself, he gave me hope. I used to have this fantasy that I'd be at a concert on the front row, thirteen years old, and in his biggest song of the night, Michael McDonald would walk to his keyboard and start playing that intro. He'd say, "I seem to have lost my voice. Is there anyone here tonight who knows the lyrics to this song, "I Keep Forgettin'?"

With my hand high in the air, I'd shout, "I know the lyrics!"

He'd see me and say, "Jeffrey Smith, would you come up here even though there are a hundred thousand people in Wembley Stadium right now, do me a favor, and just hold it down for me and sing this song in my place?"

That never happened.

Have you ever dreamed that some big event would change your life? In my dream the whole world would discover my talent and brilliance, and everything would change forever. A lot of us hold on to an idea like that. Maybe it's not as drastic as my example. Maybe it's earning a degree, or getting married, or having kids, or getting a certain kind of house, or car, or job. Many of us feel that if we reached a certain benchmark, everything would change forever. One of the most disappointing things in the world can be accomplishing one of those dreams—getting exactly what you've always wanted—and still finding something missing. Many people have lives full of big event after big event, and they are no happier than anyone else. In fact, it seems that the more you have, the more you need to sustain your happiness by getting or achieving more.

There are all kinds of potentially life-changing events, and I don't want to minimize them. Marrying Amy was one of the biggest moments in my life. The births of my children were huge events that affected me drastically, emotionally and spiritually. But they weren't magical. Life-changing moments are romanticized, and they rarely have the advertised effects.

TO LIVE IS _____

Fill in the blank. To live is _____. High-speed internet. New York-style pizza.

ONE OF THE MOST DISAPPOINTING THINGS IN THE WORLD CAN BE GETTING EXACTLY WHAT YOU'VE ALWAYS WANTED AND STILL FINDING SOMETHING MISSING.

Five-hundred-thread count Egyptian cotton sheets. We could all give a clever answer if we had a chance to clarify what's really important to us, but what if you had to choose only one word? To live is to love? To live is family? To live is to succeed? The answers would get pretty serious.

One of my favorite writers in the Bible is Paul. He filled in that blank with a really deep answer. He had a past, he was real, and he had a way with words. At one point, *he was weighing out his life* in light of the fact that people were trying to kill him for telling others about Jesus. Knowing you could die at any moment is a pretty huge thing. My friend Dave was very philosophical towards the end of his life as well, wrestling with such huge ideas. As Paul grappled with the possibility of dying or continuing to tell others about Jesus, he said, "For me, to live is Christ" (Philippians 1:21). It seems like this sentence would make more sense if it ended with an adjective. For to me, to live is awesome. For me, to live is challenging. But no, he said to live is Christ. Think about what that really means. Paul sensed that in a very short time his life could end. He was right. He was killed for preaching about Jesus. But he was contemplating what life really means when you weigh it out. His thought process looked like this. *My life is Jesus. Everything I am is because of him. Everything I do is for him. Everything I'll ever be is rushing towards him.* This doesn't mean Paul was a boring man with a myopic view of the world. It doesn't mean he didn't enjoy food and hanging out with his friends. It means that he understood his reason for living.

He goes on to say, "and to die is gain." Paul is saying, "I could live, or I could die. I'm not sure. If I live, good, then it's Jesus. If I die, in a way it's even better. I'm gaining something by dying because it's not just Jesus in my life here on earth; it's me in the presence of Jesus for all of eternity. So, to die is possibly even better. Therefore, to live is Christ, to die is gain. If they don't kill me, awesome. I'll go on living for Jesus. If they do kill me, I'll be with Jesus." But then he adds, "Yet, what will I choose?" He's asking what he prefers. It's fascinating that someone could be so confident that they could say, "I'm not even sure whether I prefer to live and keep doing all these amazing things with God, or to die, because either is fantastic." That complete peace is born out of total and absolute confidence in who Jesus is.

Don't you want that kind of peace? If you've been in pursuit of an event in your life, some moment or opportunity you think is going to change everything, you're in pursuit of something that will ultimately let you down. The only big event guaranteed to change your life is realizing you cannot live another second without letting the love of Jesus Christ be your everything.

REALLY? SOCKS?

My dad has always been my hero. He was the son of a small-town preacher. When he was eighteen, he was in a rock and roll band. He got into drugs in the sixties and was in jail facing twenty years for distribution when he came to know Jesus. He pastored many small churches when I was growing up, and eventually, my parents founded City of Life Church in central Florida in 1986, the church I took over for him in 2010. He has always been my biggest fan and my biggest encourager.

One day in 1988, I went to the mall with my friend to shop for prom. Dad gave me money to buy an outfit. In the department store my friend dared me to steal a pair of Polo socks. Maybe it was the little guy on the horse with the stick (I guess I just really dug that emblem), maybe I felt like I had something to prove, but for some reason I put those socks in my pocket. I had never stolen anything in my life. And on top of that, I had over $100 in my wallet. I was handcuffed, arrested, and taken to the Orange County jail. Grown-up jail. I called my dad, but I could only reach his secretary. She said she'd give him the message.

In forty-five minutes my dad walked up to the cell I was in, and the guard unlocked it. Any toughness I thought I had melted into tears as my dad wrapped his arms around me with a smile. The ride home was something I'll never forget. Dad didn't say anything. He just looked at me and smiled this loving, kind smile, like he wasn't mad. This made me extremely uncomfortable. I almost wanted him to be mad. Eventually, I said, "Dad, what do you think?"

The silence was killing me.

He said, "Son, that isn't you. It's not who you are."

The pain of those words was so intense I could hardly stand it. It hurt so much because I knew it was true. My parents raised me to be kind, honorable, and to never take something that wasn't mine. It hurt because he was right, but it felt good because he still believed in me.

Something about that day changed the way I looked at the world. I wanted to be the person I was supposed to be. I never wanted to let my dad down again. I never wanted to let myself down again. I certainly made many more mistakes, but in many ways that day changed who I wanted to be, affecting almost every area of my life. I had to pick up trash on the side of the road as a part of my sentence from the judge. Members of my church saw me in an orange jumpsuit. I look horrible in orange. I publically humiliated my parents. However, my dad never used either against me.

I turned to Jesus in a way I never had before. My dad demonstrated God's love toward me in such an incredible way that I felt drawn to give my whole heart to Jesus. I no longer wanted everything I used to want.

When my father affirmed me as a man who had a higher calling, I realized that my calling was to live for Jesus. I had always known that technically, but there I was in the most humiliating moment of my life, deserving every bit of shame and punishment that could possibly be thrown my way, but somehow I felt an overwhelming sense of grace and hope. Make no mistake about it—hitting rock bottom is tough. My heart goes out to everyone reading this who has been through trials and pain I could never understand.

King David was destroyed, ruined, and ashamed after losing his infant son as a result of his adulterous and murderous behavior. He acknowledged the futility of living apart from the purpose of the Lord. He wept and cried and refused to eat. Then one day, he got up and asked the Lord to give him a new heart. His focus became clear, and he determined to make God the very reason for his existence. He even asked God to use his testimony to teach wayward souls how to find their hope in the Lord.

You may not have the privilege of having an earthly father who graciously tells you that he believes in you. I will tell you with certainty, you have a heavenly Father who believes in you more than you could imagine. I don't know why we sometimes wait for tragedy to strike before we make the changes necessary to positively affect our lives. You don't have to wait for something bad to happen. Your Father loves you. He believes in you. Wherever you are in life, you can have a moment of truth.

My dad challenged me with the idea that there were two lives I could live: the one I had settled for and the unlived life within me that could only be found when I found my greatest meaning in Jesus. I found my everything in Jesus. When Paul found his everything in Jesus, he wrote it this way: "And we know that in all things God works for the good of those who love him, who have been called according to His purpose" (Romans 8:28). I'll talk about purpose a bit more in the next chapter, but I want you to know that you have been called according to his purpose.

THE BIG EVENT

There is something that happens inside when Jesus becomes your purpose in life. He doesn't help you find your purpose . . . that's the mistake we make. We think that Jesus helps us fulfill our purpose when Jesus actually wants to be our purpose. That's the point. He is our purpose. Whatever you're doing with your life right now is fine because when Jesus is your purpose, you are fully content no matter who you are and no matter what your life looks like. Jesus is not just the way to get the life you want; Jesus is the life you want. Jesus said, "I am the way the truth and the life" (John 14:6). Wow. The true destination and the path are all the same thing. Jesus.

Beyoncé is probably not going to ask you to come on stage and finish her set. Even if she did, the gratification you received would not be enough to sustain your happiness. Please don't forget the haunting words of my friend Dave. "How much time do we waste not saying the things we really mean, not doing things we really want to do, or waiting for something to happen that will really not give us the change we want?"

The big-event mentality is a lottery mentality. It's a hope that someday, somebody's going to come along and recognize you—and BOOM!—your whole life will change. Stop putting your hope and your faith in those things. Quit looking for that perfect person who's going to make your life complete. They won't. Quit looking for that house you've seen so many times you now know the entire layout, including the square footage, or that car you think you'll reward yourself with someday when you get that big promotion. Do you really think those things will make you happy?

You can have everything your heart could ever possibly desire right now, today, right this second. You have already been recognized, invited by the King himself. His purpose for you was established before you lived a day. He has placed a crown on your head and declared you royalty in the heavens. Are you really going to keep waiting for someone else to esteem you properly?

Jesus First, Jesus Always works. It's important to know that Jesus came before us. He was first. It kind of hurts your pride to realize that you are not the most important person in the universe, but it sure helps to know that the most important person in the universe loves you more than anything. I've lived this in the deep, heart-wrenching conversations I had with my friend Dave while he was dying. He struggled with life and death the way Paul did as he weighed his life against the possibility of being murdered. In Paul's discussion with the Philippians, he said, "I've considered what living means, and I've considered what dying means. To live is Christ, to die is gain. I'm not even sure which one is better." These are the conversations desperate people have. Dave told me towards the end, "I realize I have to stop waiting for some event, whether that's my healing or whatever it is. I have to start realizing that Jesus must be my everything right now, no matter what happens."

If you think there's something coming that's going to change your life for the better, you're wrong. You can't afford to wait because that big event may be a terrible event. The Big Event is already here; it's already happened, and it's staring you in the face.

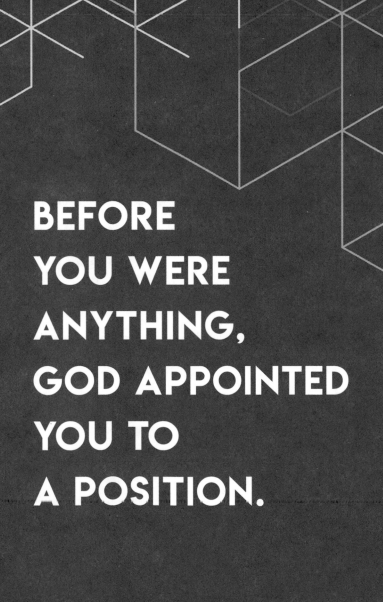

BEFORE
YOU WERE
ANYTHING,
GOD APPOINTED
YOU TO
A POSITION.

CHAPTER EIGHT:
touch the icon

"So let's go into mail. Second icon from the left on the bottom there. I just touch it with my finger, and boom, I'm there."

— Steve Jobs [4]

A MAKESHIFT LIFE

When I was sixteen, I had an '84 Thunderbird. It had little black rims on it, a bumping sound system, and a big woofer in the back. It could really get that "boom-boom" sound. The only problem was that I didn't listen to the kind of music you'd expect with a loud bass system. I drove around listening to Christopher Cross's "Sailing." It's hard to get major street cred with soft rock and a sub-woofer.

This Thunderbird was a great car, but after having it for a while, I noticed it shook when I got to 34-36 miles per hour. One mile an hour below or above that, it would be fine. But if I drove 34-36, it shook violently. Rather than getting it fixed, I just decided to go under or over that speed. I drove it that way for the longest time.

Eventually, the car also started veering and drifting. I had to hold the steering wheel crookedly in order to keep my car straight. I thought it was ruined and went to my dad. "Dad, I gotta get a new car. Buy me one. Please."

When I explained what was wrong with it, he said,

LIKE PUTTING A BANDAGE ON OVER A GASH THAT NEEDS STITCHES, WE DON'T WANT TO THINK ABOUT HOW SCREWED UP OUR LIVES REALLY ARE.

"Son, that's not a reason to buy a new car. Your alignment is off."

We took the car to the shop. The guys who knew what they were doing realigned my car, and all those problems were magically solved. I could drive as fast as I wanted! I could let go of the wheel! I did both of those things at once!

Just kidding.

In the same way, many of us have issues in our lives that we've learned to live with. We have things that don't work or are even hurting us, and rather than addressing them, we try to forget about them. Like putting a bandage over a gash that needs stitches, we don't want to think about how screwed up our lives really are. Out of sight, out of mind, right? But is that really how we're supposed to live? Putting together a makeshift life in order to be comfortable in our mess and hurt, rather than addressing the problem?

I eventually traded in my Thunderbird. I now have a sedan that's meant to cruise around and ride smooth. If I need to get around a slow car on the interstate, I step on it. It's got a little power. I like that.

I live in a city where a lot of people have four-wheelers they take off-roading. I could take my sedan that's built for the road and put it in the middle of the field, spin out, and do everything those cars are doing, but my car would probably get stuck. And it would certainly get ruined. Why? I would be using it for a purpose other than the one it was created for.

You can make most anything work in life. Some people figure out that through money, a spouse, a house, or a career they can find some level of satisfaction, but they do it apart from God. They're trying out a makeshift life, cobbling together any shred of meaning or purpose they can find. We all do this occasionally. We pick and choose things we like. We like a little bit of Jesus, a little sophisticated culture, and some pop psychology. But we can feel deep in our gut that something is still wrong, and it's the reason we're not living the life we're meant to live.

EVERYBODY RUNS

I love the movie *Minority Report*. It's based on a short story by Philip K. Dick from the 1960s. In the movie, you find these three people called precogs, which stands for precognition, who have the ability to see the future. They work together to predict crimes.

Through technology and something like wizardry, this machine spits out a ball that has the name of a person who's going to die, along with the name of the person who's going to kill them. The pre-crime division arrests someone before they commit a murder. The "killer" is put in jail prior to the murder happening because the officials know it's going to happen. It's fixed in time.

Anderton, played by Tom Cruise, learns that his own name comes up in the machine. He's going to kill someone in fewer than three days. Instead of turning himself in, he hides the prediction and runs away from

WE CAN FEEL DEEP IN OUR GUT THAT SOMETHING IS STILL WRONG, AND IT'S THE REASON WE'RE NOT LIVING THE LIFE WE'RE MEANT TO LIVE.

law enforcement. The movie becomes a cat-and-mouse chase. So good. Spielberg is brilliant.

Minority Report brings up some interesting philosophical ideas about destiny. The tagline for the movie is "Everybody runs." But is destiny something we should be running from like Anderton ran from his? Can we really run from destiny anyway? Is destiny something that's fixed, or is it something with which we have some level of involvement?

Many people have a fatalistic view of life. Someone doesn't look both ways, they step out in front of a bus, and everyone says, "Well, that was his destiny." I don't know about that. I mean, he should have looked both ways. Being hit by a bus was not necessarily destiny. Many of us get destiny very confused. Some elements of our destiny are out of our control. We don't get to choose our parents or siblings or the situations and conditions we're born into. But there's quite a bit we can control. We get to cooperate and interact with God to fulfill certain elements of our own destiny!

Some people get all caught up wondering what God's will for their lives is. Do I eat Lucky Charms or Frosted Mini Wheats for breakfast? Do I go to this college or that

WE CAN KNOW THE WILL OF GOD BY KNOWING THE WAYS OF GOD.

one? Should I get the black car or the red one? God, give me a revelation! That's not what we're talking about.

We can know the will of God by knowing the ways of God. His will is written plainly in the Bible. Scripture may not tell you what color of car to buy or what drink to get from McDonald's. It may not even tell you who to marry. But it will tell you that God's will for your life is to become like Jesus. The Ten Commandments, loving God, and loving others are some examples of the ways of God. That is called the preceptive will of God, based on the word *precept*, a principle or a rule. There's also the decretive will of

God, which is something God just decrees, and it happens. We have nothing to do with that.

We are not forced to obey the preceptive will of God, but we should do so. There should never be a moment when you say, "Oh God, please give me the wisdom to know whether I should steal from this person or not." No, the answer is no. You never have to pray about that. Why? Because not stealing is one of God's precepts. It's right there in the Bible, not to mention the laws of most civilized societies. We know the will of God in this case. If I told my son to clean his room, and he said, "Daddy, let me pray

WHEN WE CHOOSE TO LIVE OUR OWN WILL OVER GOD'S, IT ALWAYS ENDS IN PAIN.

about it," I would say, "Let me pray about letting you ever play your Wii U again. Go clean your room right now." There ain't no prayer to it. (Alabama is coming out in me.) Why? It's a precept.

God has given us the ability, but not the right, to go against his preceptive will. When we choose to live our own will over God's, it always ends in pain. It never contributes to human flourishing when we go against the preceptive will of God.

CORDIALLY INVITED

Romans 8, pound for pound, might be the most powerful chapter in the whole Bible. Many theological positions are grounded in its profound content. The word *predestined* is loaded with ideas about sovereignty and eternity. I am not only aware of this; I too find tremendous hope in the fact that God had a purpose for us before we were even born.

"And we know that in all things God works for the good of those who love him, who have been called according to his purpose. For those God foreknew he also predestined to be conformed to the image of his Son, that he might be the firstborn among many brothers and sisters. And those he predestined, he also called; those he called, he also justified; those he justified, he also glorified." (Romans 8:28–30)

And we *know that in all things, God works for the good of those who love Him.* Who is "we?" That's Christians. We know that all things work together for the good of those who love him. If you love him, then all things are working together for your good.

I love this next part. "Who have been *called.*" The Greek word for "called" here is *kletos,* which is an invitation. It's a great feeling to be invited to something, especially when someone prestigious invites you. The more prestigious the person, the higher the honor we feel. If I were to open up my mail and find an invitation saying, "Jeffrey Smith, you are invited by the President of the United States to a special banquet," I'd be pretty stoked.

Romans 8 essentially says that in all things God works for the good of those who have been *invited.* You have been given an invitation by the one who made everything, by the Alpha and Omega. We had nothing. We were nothing. We had nothing to offer. We were lost and dead in our sin. Then one day, we opened the mail to find the most beautiful invitation—the 24-karat-gold, embossed invitation, with our name on it. "You are cordially invited to a life you have never imagined, to a hope you cannot comprehend." An invitation from God. Think about that!

Another meaning of *kletos* is to be specifically appointed to an office or position—to have God, the supreme authority over all things, call you. Before you were anything, God appointed you to a position. You didn't have to have a vote from anyone. You didn't have to run for office. Because of his love for you, God specifically appointed you. All things work together for the good of those who love him, who are invited, who are called and appoint-

YOU ARE CORDIALLY INVITED TO A LIFE YOU HAVE NEVER IMAGINED, TO A HOPE YOU CANNOT COMPREHEND.

ed to a position, according to his purpose.

According to his what? The Greek word for "purpose" is *prothesis*. If you know how to break down words a bit, you know that the prefix *pro-* means "before." *Thesis* means, well, thesis—the same kind of thesis that a graduate student would write. It says, "All things work together for the good of those who love him, who are called according to his *prothesis*," his thesis, that he has proven. God stitched together something that he has proven for your life. God had a purpose for your life before you ever lived a single day. In advance, God had a dissertation he put forth about you and the way your life would look.

Moving on to verse 29, "For those God foreknew." Foreknow isn't a word we typically use, but it's pretty easy. "Fore-" is *before* something, so foreknow is to know something before it happens. It's the Greek word *proginosko*. This is where we get some of our English words. Prognosticate means basically to tell the future. A prognosis is the forecast for a disease or sickness. God foreknew people before they were ever born. Before they ever lived today, God saw into the future.

Following that concept, the Scripture says, "For those God foreknew he also predestined." The Greek word is *proorizo*, which means assigning a destiny in advance. God looked down the road, and he saw Jeffrey Smith down there. I wasn't even in existence yet, but God knew me, called me, and predestined me. Before you were ever born, God had a destiny for you that he determined about you. Here's where we go sideways. People fail to read the rest of the Scripture because people mess up when it comes to destiny. People say, "Well, my destiny is to be a doctor. My destiny is to be a husband. My destiny is to be the mother of these kids. My destiny is to be a pastor. My destiny is . . ."

Please do not confuse your vocational calling, your job, with your destiny. The two are not the same thing. Paul, the author of Romans, was a tentmaker. Nowhere in the Bible does it say that Paul's destiny was to be a tentmaker. He does talk a lot about being called and chosen for something, but it's not tents. If you're following the preceptive will of God, and you live according to the Bible, you can be a doctor. You can be a lawyer. You can be a dancer, a filmmaker, a soldier, a banker, or a real estate agent. You can do whatever you like as long as you're willing to pay the price.

If you want to be a doctor, and you're willing to go through all the years of education it takes, if you're willing to be an intern for a few years and make nothing while you have hundreds of thousands of dollars of student loans, and you have the right temperament and focus, go ahead and do it. If you don't want to be a doctor, and you want to be a singer, or a dancer, or a teacher, that's great too—again, as long as you're willing to pay the price. Teaching doesn't produce a massive yield financially, but it sows into the lives of people. As long as you're following the preceptive will of God, you could choose any number of things. Your job is not your destiny. It is your vocational calling. You're free to choose whatever vocational calling you want, as long as you're following the precepts of God.

THE "ONE"

So many people get worked up about finding "the one." Disney princess movies and chick flicks perpetuate this idea. I'm going to say probably the least romantic thing you've ever heard. "The one" doesn't exist. Somebody says, "Oh my gosh, I missed my destiny. Chase was my destiny. He was so cute. I missed him, and he married Betty instead." But Betty was supposed to marry Devin, and now Devin married the wrong person. Thanks, Chase.

You've just personally destroyed the romantic destiny of the entire planet. That's not a game of Dominoes I want to play.

I could go for a cheap re-tweet here and say, "Stop looking for the one and become the one someone is looking for," but I actually don't even believe it works like that. There are choices that you make in life—what to eat, what to wear, even who you date or marry. That is not your destiny. When you live in God's ways, what is important to God is important to you. What is attractive to God is attractive to you. He can also use circumstances conceived in sin and brokenness and redeem them with his incredible love and mercy.

Fortunately, our Scripture isn't done. There's more to say about destiny. It says, "For those God knew in advance, he also predestined." For what? To be a doctor? A lawyer? A preacher? An actor? A janitor?

No. He predestined them to be conformed. You want to know what your destiny is in this life, in this world? Your destiny is to be conformed to Jesus. What does that even mean? The Greek word is *symmorphos*. Morph, that's right. Power Rangers style.

What does it mean to morph? We're predestined

to be conformed. If you've ever seen *Terminator II*, you remember that evil terminator. The dude who goes all liquid and turns into another person. He was morphing, changing into something else.

This is your destiny—to be conformed, morphed, into the image of Christ. Want more Greek? The word for "image" is *eicon*. If you pronounce that *E* with an *I*, what do you get? Our destiny is to be conformed into the icon of Jesus. This is huge!

CLINT EASTWOOD: AMERICAN ICON

Icon has multiple meanings. One definition is someone who represents an entire field of something. They alone represent a whole genre. Clint Eastwood is an icon of the movie industry. He's a phenomenal director. He's acted in movies. He's written screenplays. He's produced. He is an icon. To understand the movie industry, all you really need to understand is Clint Eastwood because he represents the whole thing. Do you understand the implications? Your destiny is to be so transformed from what you used to be into the icon of Jesus that you *become* the icon of Jesus.

In the Eastern Orthodox tradition, Christians med-

YOUR DESTINY IS TO BE A WINDOW TO GOD FOR SOMEONE ELSE.

itate on icons—pictures or depictions of Jesus or other saints—with the expectation that those icons will direct them to God. Icons are windows to God. Your destiny is to be a *window* to God for someone else.

Look at your phone for a second. Play with a couple of your apps for a minute. Go ahead and check your social media, then come back. I'll wait.

How did you get into your apps?

You touched the icon. That one tiny little picture is a representation of the entire application that the developer designed for you. That icon is the way into the app. You do not open an application through an icon and accidentally get things that are contrary to it. In fact, when you open it, the only things that show up are the things that are relevant to that app and icon. Touch the Candy Crush icon, and you're not going to get Clash of the Clans. The only thing you'll get is Candy Crush.

Your destiny is to be transformed into a window, an icon, a hyperlink. Have you ever been browsing around a webpage, and something of this nature shows up? "Make sure you sign up for this program!" The phrase *sign up* is highlighted. What do you do? You click on the phrase, and the hyperlink takes you to a page where you don't have to search for the sign-up. It's just there. Our destiny is to be conformed to be the hyperlink of Jesus. We become the icon. When someone comes in contact with me, they shouldn't have to search for Jesus. I should be the window to Jesus. They should be able to recognize the icon that I claim to be.

Romans 8:29 says that Jesus is the firstborn among a large family. Our pre-destiny that God foreknew and fore-saw before we were ever born is that we would be trans-formed into the image, the icon, the hyperlink, of Jesus in order that we become his brother or sister. He's still the highest among all of us. He is the Alpha and Omega, after all. But the Bible tells us that we are co-heirs with Christ. God gives us the same level of honor that he's given to Jesus! And this honor isn't something we earned. It's not based on us. It's based on God's grace and love for us.

God has called you to this. Another meaning for *kletos* is "to name." God has named you for this. "Those that he predestined, he also named" (Romans 8:30). God is saying that everything you are will be embodied in that name. He's calling you. Those he predestined, he also named.

Those he called and named, he also justified, *dikaios*, which means "to render righteous." God looked at you and your future when you were nothing. He took his gavel of justice and said, "I render them not guilty." Only God would give a verdict before any behavior has occurred.

God foreknew you. God predestined and called you, naming you to be conformed to the image, the icon, the hyperlink, of Jesus. God has justified you, rendered you righteous because of Jesus. And because you are justified, God has glorified you.

The word for "glorified" is *doxazo*. A doxology is a song of praise to God. It's glory. It's honor. This Scripture is saying that God honored us, praised us, made us

WHEN YOU'RE CONFORMED TO THE IMAGE OF JESUS, YOU'RE LIVING YOUR DESTINY.

co-heirs—brothers and sisters—with Jesus. Not only did God name us, not only did he render us righteous, but he also gave us honor. As Jesus' brother or sister, co-heir, you inherit his glory.

If you're reading this today with low self-esteem, forget that. We're talking about *destiny*. We're talking about Jesus First, Jesus Always. Jesus First because he came before you and did all this before you were born. Many people are oblivious to their destiny, but our destiny is right here in the Bible. It's that obvious. Live your life in a way that your destiny is obvious to you. Your destiny is to be the icon of Jesus.

You don't have to finish

a course or have a degree. You don't have to be married to a certain person or have a certain house or car. You can fulfill your destiny today, right in this moment, because it is to be conformed to the image of Jesus. When you're conformed to the image of Jesus, you're living your destiny.

Maybe you've been oblivious to your destiny. Or maybe you think you've missed out on it, so you're living Plan B or C, a makeshift life that's devoid of purpose and meaning. Thank God, it's not like that. You can attain your destiny, right here and now.

This life is about him. Several times in the book of Psalms, David asks the Lord to keep him under the shadow of his wings. Besides how lovely that sounds, it is a brilliant revelation that Jesus *overshadows* us. Living a life overshadowed by someone else sounds pretty contrary to everything people are after these days. David understands that there is wisdom, safety, and protection under the shadow of Jesus. When he becomes *first, always,* and *everything in between,* we gain a perspective previously unimaginable: I shine brighter in the shadow of Jesus than I could ever shine in my own limelight.

You can conform to the image of Jesus. You can be the icon of Jesus wherever you go, the hyperlink that allows people to experience God in their own lives. What purpose or calling could be greater or more fulfilling than that? In a broken world where people are desperately groping around in the darkness for purpose, turning to anything that offers fulfillment, people don't need to meet another Jesus groupie. They don't need another admirer. They need an icon.

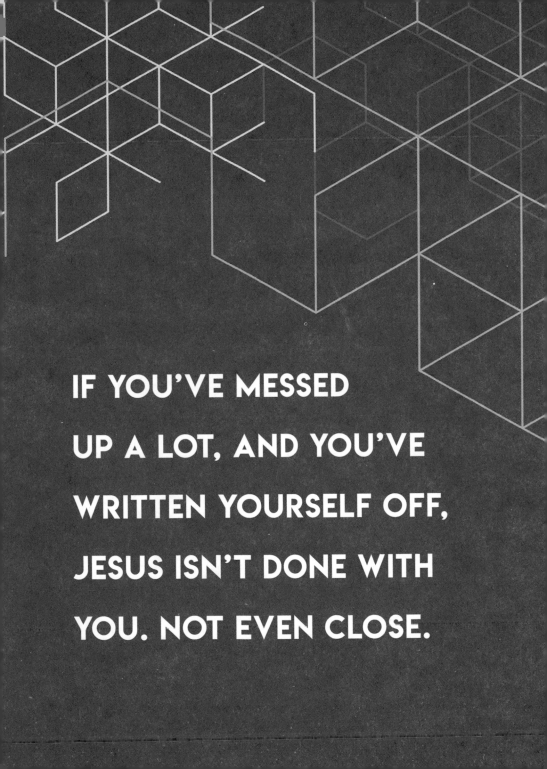

IF YOU'VE MESSED
UP A LOT, AND YOU'VE
WRITTEN YOURSELF OFF,
JESUS ISN'T DONE WITH
YOU. NOT EVEN CLOSE.

CHAPTER NINE:

it's gonna be different

"Therefore, if anyone is in Christ, the new creation has come: The old has gone, the new is here!"

— **2 Corinthians 5:17**

THE LEITMOTIF IS NO LIGHT MOTIF

I love music. When I was two years old, my parents used to stand me on the piano to sing with them in churches all over America. After high school, I became a recording artist and music producer for nearly twenty years. I've had the opportunity to write and record with some of the greatest artists around. I've even had a chance to do some scoring for films.

As you can probably tell, I also love movies—so much

so that I've even had the opportunity to try my hand at directing. I've directed many short films, and I'm currently working on several feature films for the future. One thing I've learned about filmmaking is that music is important to a movie—it can make or break it. I've seen bad movies with great scores that were enjoyable because the music was so good. Conversely, I've seen well-made films with awful music that made the movie nearly unbearable.

One important element of music in film is something called the leitmotif. Used in all the best movie scores, it's a musical theme intended to create an emotional attachment to a character or element of the movie. It's a tune associated with a specific person, place, or idea that recurs as an integrated part of a plot.

The brilliant composer John Williams cornered the market when it comes to the leitmotif. Think about the music in *Jaws*. I know people who were scared to get into a pool after seeing that movie because of the music! When I was ten I was one of them. Why? Because the leitmotif conveys fear. What about the theme song from *Raiders of the Lost Ark*? When you hear it, you can see Indiana Jones with his leather jacket, his fedora, and trademark whip hanging off the side of a moving truck. Why? Because the leitmotif conveys adventure.

The guy who really developed the idea of the leitmotif was German composer Richard Wagner, whose operas were referred to as music dramas. In order to bring his characters to life, he created a dramatic musical phrase for each character that helped drive the plot. Without Wagner, film scores wouldn't be the same today. When we hear the *Chariots of Fire* theme song, everything turns into a slow-mo running montage. The trumpets in the *Rocky* theme song get hearts pumping a little faster, and we want to fight someone. And who's Darth Vader without "The Imperial March"? Music is just that

THROUGHOUT JESUS'S STORY IN SCRIPTURE, WE SEE THE SAME RECURRING THEME, I LOVE YOU JUST THE WAY YOU ARE.

powerful.

If Jesus' life were a movie, it would have a powerful score. And Jesus would definitely have a leitmotif. Throughout his story in Scripture, we see the same recurring theme. *I love you just the way you are* is found throughout the whole Bible, beginning with creation in Genesis and ending with recreation in Revelation. You should hear and feel the leitmotif of Jesus all around you because he has a theme—love. We see time and time again that Jesus' radical love transforms people. We see over and over people leaving behind what they previously knew and chasing after the one thing that matters.

ELEVEN LEPERS, THREE RESPONSES

In our current Western culture, the disease once known as leprosy has all but been eradicated. Since most people are generally unfamiliar with its symptoms or social ramifications, let me explain a little bit about what we now call Hansen's Disease. Leprosy is a disease that causes a person to gradually lose all sensitivity to touch. Say someone had to grip a tool, or they cut themselves while working. They would not be able feel the pain at all. They'd have gashes and cuts on their bodies. They could be cooking and pick something up without realizing that their own hand was burning. Body parts could fall off. Otherwise-painful infections could spread because people were too numb to realize their presence. It's a devastating kind of disease. Back in the days when there was no cure, it was a death sentence.

Isn't that how it is with all of us, though? Sometimes we become so numb we no longer have the sensibilities to know that we are hurting ourselves. Our broken soul can become so desensitized that we get cut, burned, and scarred, whether it be through substance abuse, identity issues, sex, materialism, the pursuit of fame or success, whatever. We lose our sensitivities that tell us those things are deeply hurting us.

All of us are unclean without Jesus. Not just the people in this story. You, me, your parents, your siblings, and your best friend. But Jesus offers the healing we need. Jesus offers a new way of living, free of guilt and shame.

THE DESPERATE ONE

Jesus loves desperate people. I'm thankful for that because

ARE YOU READY FOR SOME- THING NEW IN YOUR LIFE?

it means he loves me. The book of Mark tells a story about a social outcast who had no other hope but Jesus: "A man with leprosy came to him and begged him on his knees, 'If you choose, you can make me clean.' Moved with pity, Jesus stretched out his hand and touched him, and said to him, 'I do choose. Be made clean!' Immediately the leprosy left him, and he was made clean" (Mark 1:40–42).

The leper came to Jesus. I know the rules about leprosy in that culture. Lepers weren't allowed to come to anyone. They were quarantined. Once when I was in Nigeria, my group passed by a leper colony. Cut off from society, they couldn't see their families or friends. We got to play music for them and spend time with them. They were so sweet and happy to see us. In Jesus' time, they would have had to shout from a distance. In fact, in order to let other people know that a leper was in their midst, lepers had to yell out "Unclean! Unclean!" as they passed by. This guy is so sick of his situation, he's willing to break all the rules to get his miracle!

Are you sick of your situation, tired of the way things have been? Are you ready for something new in your life? Are you willing to do what this man did—break out of your comfort zone and approach Jesus?

In our culture, we absolutely don't like to admit mistakes. Most of the time we can barely admit our struggles. The leper came to Jesus, though, begging. He was so desperate. Kneeling down, he humbled himself before Jesus and said, "If you are willing . . ." What an act of faith. Do you believe Jesus has the ability to make you clean no matter what you have done in your life or will do?

We have to be willing to fall at Jesus' feet, be vulnerable with God, and say, "I believe with all of my heart that you will take me as I am, in my broken condition. I believe you have the power to heal me." If you've messed up a lot, and you've written yourself off, Jesus isn't done with you. Not even close.

I love Jesus' response. Jesus is moved with compassion. Jesus is compassionate toward your situation too. He doesn't just feel it. It moves him. As a matter of fact, the word here, *splagchnizomai*, means "move with compassion." It's a Greek word. No one will want to be naming their kid that anytime soon, but *splagchnizomai* means getting fired up. Another translation means literally that your heart flips upside down in your chest when someone says something.

One time my son, Jude, after I'd explained to him what offerings were, wanted to give. He looked up at me with all the innocence of a child and said, "Daddy, I want to give an offering. Do you think this will be enough?" He held out a quarter.

Right then and there, my heart broke. I was like, "Of course. Anything you give with a heart like that is enough for God." It was so cute and sweet, and my heart was moved with compassion. My heart flipped upside down.

When God looks at your situation, he's not pointing his finger at you. He is moved with compassion. His heart flips upside down for you. Jesus heard this man say, "Jesus, if you're willing." And he was more than willing. Jesus is thinking, right now, *You have no idea how willing I am to help you. I've been waiting your whole life for this moment.* "Moved with compassion, he stretched out his hand and he said to him" (now, the Bible omitted this part you're about to read, but I'm sure it was probably there) "Oh, yeah, I am willing. Be cleansed." That's what Jesus is saying to you today. Whatever you have gone through, Jesus is willing to help you right now.

Think about a different story in Luke 17. Ten lepers were hanging out together. They followed the rules, so they were outside of the city gates, and they called out to Jesus from afar. They yelled, "Hey, Master! Can you help us out? Anything you can do for us over here? Have pity on us, dude!" He called back, "Hey, yeah, go show yourself to the priests." That's it. That's the only real interaction that took place between them. They asked for help, he sent them to the priest, and off they went to the temple. We don't get a lot of other narrative that might make it really cool. We know they were like, "Alright, whatever" and started walking to the temple. We don't know who was healed first. We don't know when the healing occurred, if it occurred simultaneously, or slowly. Maybe one guy was walking along and said, "Yeah, I think—oh my gosh! My hand! Hey, Bill, does that look normal to you? Holy cow!" We don't know. What we do know is that one of them, when he saw he was healed, came back praising God in a loud voice.

THE THANKFUL ONE

A loud voice. Ain't nobody whispering when they get healed of leprosy. Sometimes you just need to praise God in a loud voice. You might need to do that right where you are now. For real, mark the page and thank God in a loud voice for all he's done for you. There's something about that kind of gratitude that moves God.

It also says, "He threw himself at Jesus' feet and thanked him." I was preaching this message in my church not long ago, and on the second row were five sharp-looking guys who were really into my message. They were all in their early twenties with some of the coolest tattoo work I've seen in a while. They were nodding and saying "Amen" really loud, so I decided to invite one guy on stage. I said, "I like you guys. I don't know who you are, but would one of y'all come up here? I need a volunteer."

This tall guy came up, and he looked really nervous. I told him he may not be an actor, but I'd like him to demonstrate what it might look like to throw yourself at Jesus' feet. I explained that in order to do this effectively he'd have to imagine the feeling of taking every broken thing in his life, every failure, everything that's not right.

He stopped me. "I've got it man—it's vivid, it's vivid."

I said, "You've finally found the one person who can forgive you."

This guy's eyes were filling with tears, causing me to get emotional as well. When I told him to fall at Jesus feet, he lunged toward "Jesus" and cried out with a loud voice, "Jesus, please forgive me." Later in the service this young man and all his friends from a local drug and alcohol rehabilitation center committed their lives to following Jesus. Jesus First, Jesus Always. While onstage, he wasn't pretending. He was experiencing forgiveness and the love of Jesus for the very first time. No wonder the church was on its feet going crazy.

The man at my church fell at Jesus' feet, just like the thankful leper. He laid down on his face, saying, "Thank you so much for your mercy, your grace, your goodness. You've taken everything I used to be and washed it away."

This man is thankful. Are you thankful for what God has delivered you from?

THE UNGRATEFUL ONES

So now we understand the thankful one, but we've also got the nine guys who were healed but never came back. These guys just took off with all this blessing. On the way to the priest, they were healed. That's all we know.

I think the other nine probably came up with some excuses on the way to the temple. "Maybe we were misdiagnosed in the first place." "It's just a coincidence." "If he's really the Messiah, he's all-knowing, and he'll know we're grateful." "Think about it guys, we were feeling better already."

But one came back. And he threw himself at the feet of Jesus and worshiped.

Let me just tell you something about the ungrateful ones, though. As weak sauce as it is that they didn't say "thank you," we don't hear an addendum to the story where it says, "And nine of them did their own thing. They didn't follow what Jesus asked them to do, so Jesus snapped his fingers and, boom, they had leprosy again." Jesus isn't like that. I gotta give these guys credit. At least they had enough sense to obey Jesus at first. Scripture tells us, "As they went, they were healed." It was a process. *As they went.*

I think in these three different responses to Jesus, we learn three key points about how God heals us all.

1. God heals us all in different ways.

My dad grew up in church, had a traumatic event in his life, turned to sex, drugs, and rock and roll. He was even in a band that opened for the Rolling Stones. He got busted and faced twenty years in the penitentiary for pushing cocaine. His life looked like it was over, and in the middle of a jail cell, he accepted Jesus in 1969.

The power of God came into that jail cell. The judge dropped all the charges and gave him a sentence of preaching to high schools. Over the years, my dad has had a few LSD flashbacks, random hallucinations because of drugs he did before he came to Christ, but his heart and life have been completely transformed.

My story is not his story. I loved Jesus when I was growing up. All the stuff I did, I did knowing the love and acceptance of Jesus. I'm more of a moron than my father was. My mistakes have been blatant, and there are many times I wished I had a different story, but I don't.

Your story is not his story. Your story is not my story. God heals us all in different ways. It's why Jesus, when he healed blind people, deliberately healed them differently. He didn't want them to get attached to the wrong thing, the method of healing. In some instances, Jesus laid hands on people and—boom!—they were healed. One time, he spit in the dirt, mixed it up, made a little clay, and stuck it on a guy's eyes and—boom!—he was healed. In another instance, Scripture says Jesus just walks up to some dude, says, "Hey, man, what's up," and spits in his eyes. I mean, this guy's

WE DON'T NEED TO FOCUS ON THE METHOD; WE NEED TO FOCUS ON THE MESSIAH. HE'S THE ONE WHO HEALS.

like, "Hey, what's up? Jesus, is that you? Whoa, *did you just spit in my eye?*" Then suddenly he's seeing. Another time Jesus doesn't even touch the guy. He just *tells* him he's healed. Jesus does it all in different ways.

Why didn't Jesus heal people with clay every single time? Because he knew we can be really stupid. Someone somewhere would have a church called First Church of the Clay Spittle, and they'd base their whole life and ministry around the method Jesus used to heal one person, rather than on Jesus himself. We don't need to focus on the method; we need to focus on the Messiah. He's the one who heals us.

2. God heals us all at different times.

God also heals us at different times. The leper in the first story came to Jesus. He was earnest. He implored Jesus, and the Scripture says that when Jesus laid hands on him, he was immediately healed. After the healing took place, Jesus told him to show himself to the priest. He gave him some lifestyle change. Jesus told the man what to do, but after he was already healed.

Jesus told the group of ten lepers to change their lifestyle—go to the priest—and in the process of obeying

GO AND GIVE.

GO AND SERVE.

GO AND STUDY.

GO AND PRAY.

GO AND WORSHIP.

what Jesus said, they were healed.

God heals us at different times. Maybe you had a powerful encounter with God, and it immediately transformed you. Your life has never been the same. Or maybe you're reading today, you've been serving God for years, and you're still waiting for that Big Event. I'll remind you again—the Big Event is Jesus.

The greatest miracle you have is your salvation in Jesus and the promise of paradise, being with Him. That can never be taken away from you. Someday in the future, even if you never have some huge moment, you'll look back and be amazed at the work God has done in your life. You won't be the same as you are today. God heals us in different ways. He heals us at different times.

3. God always sets us on a different path.

Jesus told both groups of people—the single leper and the ten lepers—"Go." Whatever you've been doing up to this point, wherever you've been, obviously hasn't helped you. He's saying, "Go from where you are to where you're supposed to be. Get away from that old life. Get into the new life."

Do what Jesus is telling you to do today. Go and give. Go and serve. Go and study. Go and pray. Go and worship. Get away from what doesn't work and start doing what does work. Situate your life in Christ—Jesus First, Jesus Always. You never found a miracle the old way, so start living the new way. Scripture says, "As they went, they were cleansed" (Luke 17:14). They were healed on the new path.

In 2 Kings 5, a leper named Naaman went to see a prophet of God named Elisha to be healed. He wasn't even a believer in God, but he wanted to see what all the fuss was about. Elisha told him to dip seven times in the

Jordan River. He said, "You want to be healed? Here's the process."

Instead of going through the process, Naaman left angry. He griped to everybody around him. "Oh, I thought Elisha was a man of God. Why couldn't he just say, 'Boom—you're healed'? That's exactly what I envisioned in my head—that he was going to say, 'Boom.'" A lot of people think when they come to Jesus he's going to say, "Boom—your marriage is fixed, Boom—you're a millionaire, Boom—everything you ever wanted is right in front of you."

One of Namaan's assistants was with him and said, "Why don't you just listen to him? He told you to go dip. Just go dip. Do you want to be healed or not?"

Namaan was like, "Fine. One, two, three, four . . ."

Wouldn't you know, on the seventh time this man came up, the Bible says that his skin looked like the skin of a little boy. He had brand new skin when he came up that last time.

God heals us differently and at different times, but God always sets us on a path. There's always a next step. There's always a process. Submit to the process. Lean into it.

Can you hear the leitmotif of Jesus? Listen closely. Its rhythm and melody are surrounding you with hope for tomorrow because you will never be stuck in hopelessness. Its harmonies blend who you are with who you are becoming in him. Its chorus triumphantly declares that your future in him is more wonderful than you could possibly imagine.

GOD HEALS US DIFFERENTLY AND AT DIFFERENT TIMES, BUT GOD ALWAYS SETS US ON A PATH.

JESUS DIDN'T COME TO ERASE OUR PAST. HE CAME TO REDEEM IT.

CHAPTER TEN:
live to tell

"I believe every Christian needs to know that they are not only saved, but are also called to live a life of purpose."
— **Brian Houston**[5]

FOCUS

Have you ever noticed a really cool new car for the first time and actually liked it enough to go to a dealership and test drive it? You love this car. It's not just any car—if you bought this car, it would show your taste, your efficiency, your regard for the environment . . . basically it would validate your style and originality to all who shall behold it.

You sit in it. You envision yourself winning at *life* in this car. It drives better than you had anticipated. The technology is ten years ahead of its time. You start doing the mental calculations on what you will have to shift around in your budget to buy this car. The car salesman offers a variety of creative ways you can finance it. You make your decision. You buy the car.

You drive off the lot feeling confident you have made one of the best decisions of your life. No sooner than when you pull out of the parking lot, though, you see the same car sitting at a red light next to you. You think, *That's odd, I've never seen that kind of car in my life until yesterday. Well, we are near the dealership. That person probably works here.* You proceed to drive home and notice another car like yours pass you, coming from the opposite direction. Then you pull in your driveway and notice that your neighbor owns the same car. This continues from now on. How did so many people become interested in the same car you noticed on the same day you decided you were going to buy it?

What is that?

It happens in other areas too. You are reading a book, and you come across a word you have never seen. Let's say that word is "schadenfreude." You are intrigued and decide to actually open a dictionary and look up its meaning.

Scha•den•freu•de: *pleasure derived by someone from anoth-*

er person's misfortune

This explains why you might enjoy watching a You-Tube video of someone attempting to push another person into a pool but only falling in themselves. You have now learned a new word. At dinner that night with a few friends, someone is telling a story about getting the very last ticket to a huge Broadway show at the box office, and they felt *schadenfreude* as they were walking away looking at all the people in line who would be unable to get tickets. You notice the word *instantly*, yet everyone at the table laughs and nods. Everyone knows that word. You say, "Yeah, schadenfreude" just so it appears you have known that word your whole life, yet you secretly are thinking, *How am I the only person here who didn't know that word until today?* Now you hear that word on television, in coffee shops . . . it even seems children know it.

What is that?

My mom is a brilliant psychologist, and when she was working on her dissertation in 2002 she shared a concept with me that blew my mind. There is a netlike formation of neurons in our brainstem called the Reticular Activating System (RAS). It is a system that not only regulates wakefulness and sleep-wake transitions, but it also actually filters information and regulates alertness and attention. Consider it the attention center of the brain. If you have ever wondered how our brain is able to process billions of pieces of information at any given moment and decide which ones are important and which ones are not, this is the answer.

RAS is the reason we are able to walk through an airport with so much going on all around us: the sound of employees scanning tickets, people on their computers, hundreds of voices filling the air, Starbucks coffee being made (yeah that made me thirsty too), the guy talking into his jawbone as if the person he is talking to is literally two thousand miles away. All of these things are going on, yet a voice comes on the intercom and says, "Jeffrey Smith, please come to the ticket counter at gate 72", and you actually hear it. You notice. In the middle of chaos, you recognize your name. Why? RAS has just discovered something that is pertinent to your mission, to your purpose, to what you're trying to accomplish. In the simplest form, we have something hardwired into our brains that keeps us in line with our purpose.

If this is true, it brings up a pretty significant question. How does our brain know what our purpose is? Some of it is very primal—things like keeping us out of danger—but if RAS is trying to keep us on mission, how can we establish what the mission is? A great deal of that has to do with what you value and focus on at a core level. People who are focused on happiness are subconsciously trying to find stimuli that support what they are committed to on a deep level. Have you ever noticed that people who complain about being unhappy generally stay that way? I'm truly not just talking about the power of positivity here; I'm talking about the fact that on a scientific level we determine what is important to us, we embed that in our coding, and RAS helps us achieve it by focusing on what is crucial to our mission.

When Paul says, "to live is Christ," he is saying that life is *simply Jesus*. If *Jesus First, Jesus Always* is the purpose of my life, I will focus on things that are crucial to my mission. My spiritual RAS will help filter things out that do not help me. When Jesus becomes the very thing in your life that you live for, he becomes your ultimate reward, your reason for living. Accomplishment is not what you're seeking. He is what you're seeking. You're not seeking approval from anyone. You're seeking to know Jesus. To live is Christ, to die is gain. Something happens deep within you, and you begin to drown out everything in your life that is not important. While everyone else is complaining about "the struggle" or fawning over the latest trend, your heart and your spirit starts to say, "I don't even have to worry about that. That's not important to my mission. I'm only going to worry about things that are important to my mission." Now you are on track.

So what happens when your spiritual RAS is fine-tuned? You hear a message of hope. Instead of writing it off—boom! That's part of my mission. You get good news. Instead of reasoning it away or chalking it up to coincidence—boom! That's part of my mission. You meet people who need encouragement in life and can tell from the way they talk that they are not coming up with any answers—boom! That's part of my mission, my purpose. You start noticing things that matter.

Get your focus right. Drown out the noise and the insignificant voices that desperately try to distract you from your mission. Concentrate on your purpose in this life. No *schadenfreude* could be as gratifying as having so much focus that you are able to actually help others find their purpose in life.

See? RAS works after all.

When Jesus becomes your everything, you are looking for ways to make his hope known to others. Part of your purpose becomes helping others find their purpose. After all, how can you keep such great news a secret?

When Jesus healed people, he usually told them to go and tell no one. Isn't that strange? "You've been blind your whole life, and now you can actually see, but, uh, don't tell anyone." Really? When something life-changing happens to me, the first thing I want to do is tell someone. If something is confidential, I'll never tell a soul, but when I'm excited about something, I'm the worst secret-keeper ever. I can barely keep a secret when I buy Amy a surprise gift. I can't imagine having my life forever changed by the Son of God and then being told that I'm not allowed to share my story. Why would Jesus tell people that?

For starters, Jesus did most of his ministry in a very small region, and there were a lot of religious leaders who hated him. The more people found out about his power, the more difficult it would be for him to love and help people the way he needed to.

Remember when Jesus prayed for the man who was posessed by demons? This guy was *violent*. He hurt himself and others. . Needless to say, this guy was an outcast. When Jesus prayed for him, though, the man became completely peaceful—a different person, nothing like he used to be. He even asked Jesus if he could come along with him. Jesus broke this man's pattern when he told him, "Go home to your own people and tell them how much the Lord has done for you, and how he has had mercy on you" (Mark 5:19). The advice Jesus was giving this newly freed man was significantly different than his advice to others. Jesus was foreshadowing here what our lives look like when we too have been set free. Jesus now wants all of us to share what God has done for us. We don't have to soften our past, rewrite it, or pretend it didn't happen.

Jesus didn't come to erase our past. He came to redeem it.

There is a difference between bragging about mistakes you've made and using them as a way of honoring God's love. You are not just loved by God. You are loved as much as it is possible to be loved. And you are loved that much on your worst day. That's a love worth telling someone about.

SHARE YOUR STORY

When I was eight years old, my dad took me out on a

night fishing trip with a bunch of guys we knew. Though Florida is not known for cold weather, it was about forty degrees, and I was bundled up for the trip. When we got to the loading area, there was a huge boat about seven feet from the edge of the dock. The strangest thing happened to me when I looked at that boat. My heart started to beat out of my chest, my palms got sweaty, I started breathing heavily, and I got a jolt of adrenaline. I thought to myself, *I can make that jump*. I leaned forward, and my dad tapped me on the shoulder and said, "Boy, don't you even think about trying to make that jump." I dissuaded his fears instantly. "No way . . . I was just messing around."

I lied.

I had every intention of transforming into the Six Million Dollar Man and launching myself as far into the air as possible. I took off like a rocket. I timed the jump to perfection. My toes hit the very edge of the dock, skillfully accelerating my body skyward in what appeared to be a world-record jump. I was almost there when I dropped straight down. Like a rock. I landed in the freezing water and thought I was going to die. Dad climbed down and pulled me out of the water. (I do not suggest going night fishing in nearly freezing temperatures.) I sat under a towel shivering and embarrassed most of the night. I missed the mark . . . big time.

Sometimes when I share my story with people, it seems really difficult to connect, and I flat-out miss the mark. After all, not everyone shares my same interests in life. Have you ever met someone who you just did not get along with? I know that doesn't sound very spiritual, but am I the only one here? It's like you meet them, and nothing clicks. I don't know why that happens, but every once in a while, I run into someone like that.

Not long ago, I was on a flight from Orlando to Los Angeles. That six-hour flight is so long sometimes. I try to sleep for the first part—an hour or two—and then I'll watch a movie. I'll try (unsuccessfully) to read, and there are still three hours left. On this particular flight, I was trying to kill some time, so I thought, *Maybe I'll talk to this dude sitting next to me.* I said, "Hey man, how are you doing?"

He said, "I'm great."

"I'm great too." *We've got a whole connection going on here. I'm great; you're great.* "Are you from Orlando?"

"Oh, God, no. I hate Orlando. Where are you from?"

"I live in Orlando. Why do you hate Orlando? Orlando has Disney."

"Oh, I hate Disney."

"You hate Disney?"

"Yes, I hate Disney."

"Why do you hate Disney?"

"Because I'm a grown-up."

"I'm a grown-up, and I love Disney." *Oh, this is going perfectly.* "Okay, do you like music?"

He said, "I hate music."

"You hate music? What do you hate—the commercialization of music, or what? You hate music?"

"Yes, I hate music."

"Well, do you like movies?"

"I love movies."

I said, "Yes!" There was a slight pause.

"Ah, but movies have music in them," I said.

"Yeah, but it's only there to underscore the story."

"Do you like musical movies?"

"Can't stand them."

"So, uh, you don't like *Grease*?"

"That's a great movie."

"But *Grease* has a lot of music in it."

"I hate the music in *Grease*, but I love Olivia Newton John."

Aha. I also love Olivia Newton John. Now we are best friends, and I'm going to use this to somehow share my story.

I'm sure it doesn't come as a surprise, but it didn't work very well in this instance. I tried. Thankfully, opportunities arise time and time again, so not long after, I found myself at a conference in Newport Beach. Of all places in the world, I ended up at a car wash. (Who washes a rental car? Apparently I do when I'm taking some friends out for dinner, and somehow the company rented me a car that was filthy!) I was waiting for my car to be detailed and got into a conversation with a very nice lady. We talked for almost ten minutes, and she asked me what I did for a living. I told her I was a pastor, and she said, "Wow, I've never met one of you before." She proceeded to tell me that she had been raised as an atheist, but because of our conversation, she was now interested in my beliefs. She said, "I'll tell you what, I'm going to give you five minutes to convince me to become a Christian. Go."

Suddenly, I was not a pastor, I did not think of my PhD in theology or how many messages I've delivered in my life. I was that eight-year-old boy staring down the dock with adrenaline pumping through my body. My hands started sweating, my heart started to race, and I remembered the outcome I suffered in that icy water. I felt the Lord speak to my heart and say, "You can never fall on your face, only into grace." It was exactly what I needed, and it rhymed. I did my best to tell my story and explain why Jesus was my everything. I told her he was my first, my always, and everything in between. I told her about stupid things I'd done and how God never gave up on me. Then my five minutes were up. I was hoping for tears, but that didn't happen. She flatly said, "My car is done. This is crazy. I came for a car wash, and now I'm headed to a bookstore to buy a Christian Bible. I'm going to read it cover to cover."

I used to compare my story to all of these wild testimonies, and I felt inadequate. My story is not amazing because of the craziness of what I used to do; it's amazing because God has redeemed it.

Your story, regardless of what it is, is powerful because God has redeemed it. And God will use your past to change someone else's future.

You have been truly redeemed. Shame has no claim on you anymore because God has set you free.

2 Corinthians 5:17 says, "Therefore, if anyone is in Christ, the new creation has come. The old has gone, the

new is here!"

I don't ever want to lose that adrenaline, that feeling you get when you know you have an opportunity to give someone hope. That feeling means I can't do it on my own, but I'm not alone. Immanuel is here to help me.

God has not erased your past. God has redeemed your past. So many people want to go back, but God wants to put finality to the things in our past. He doesn't come with an eraser and say, "You were never abused" or "You never cheated on anyone." He doesn't say, "You never lied. You never caused this massive drama in your life." He says, "You did everything you did, and

HE USES YOUR WHOLE STORY— THE GOOD THE BAD, AND THE UGLY, THE MAJOR EVENTS AND THE SEEMINGLY USELESS STUFF.

I have redeemed it all. I have set you free from the guilt, shame, and pain of your past."

But God doesn't just redeem your mistakes. He uses your *whole* story—the good, the bad, and the ugly, the major events and the seemingly useless details. Maybe you're reading this, and you have a pretty good life, or maybe it all just seems pointless. Maybe you went to college or got a Master's degree in an area you don't work in. You had a path in your life that you thought was going to be your whole world, and then you ended up doing something completely different. Do you believe it was all for nothing? Not if you believe God has redeemed your past.

Redeem is a great word. According to Merriam-Webster's Online Dictionary, it means "to buy back; to free from captivity by payment of ransom: to release from blame or debt; to change for the better." We say, "Those were the lost years, the years I can never get back." But God wants to redeem your whole past. He wants to use all the experiences you've ever had to equip you to reach people in the future.

Let's take a look at King David. Theologians believe he may have been the most gifted and talented songwriter, singer, and musician who ever lived. He was prolific, just writing all the time. But he was also a young shepherd, in charge of his family's sheep, who hung out by himself in the middle of nowhere. He didn't even get to be with human beings. He was with animals all the time.

Picture David writing songs in front of animals. "Thank you, guys, for showing up today. Here comes the concert. I got this new jam I want to break off for you all. It's called 'The Lord is my Shepherd.' I have a feeling it's going to be popular in the future." Maybe he thought, *What am I doing? I am wasting my time.* Then a bear comes to attack the sheep. Bam!—he kills the bear. Another time a lion tries to attack the sheep. He kills the lion. He's learning how to do combat. An opportunity comes up when an enemy is coming against Israel. And what does he do? He slays Goliath with the same skills he developed while being a shepherd.

What happens to David? The prophet Samuel anoints him King of Israel. He becomes the shepherd over the whole flock of Israel, and he leads them as a king. God uses David to shepherd Israel and defeat Goliath. And those songs he wrote? Yeah, check out Psalms.

How about Moses? Baby Moses was found floating down the river in a basket. Pharaoh's daughter picks him up and raises him in royalty. He's a Jew, but he's raised as an Egyptian prince. When Moses grows up, he kills someone in anger and then flees Egypt to a place called Midian, a land where he's a nobody, and becomes a shepherd for forty years. *Forty years.* You're talking about a sophisticated, highly-educated, combat-trained man, and he's living with animals for forty years. God uses his education to help him negotiate with Pharaoh later in life. And what about those forty years spent in the wilderness of Midian as a shepherd? He needed every one of those years of experience because for forty *more* years he would shepherd God's people in the wilderness. God used his past to transform others' futures.

What about the apostle Peter? Before he was a disciple, he was just a rough-around-the-edges fisherman. Fishermen spit and cuss and just like being dudes. It's kind of fun to be around fishermen because they don't care. That's the kind of people Jesus chose. You don't have to have it all together for Jesus to use you. He just walks up to these guys and says, "Hey, follow me." When Peter finally realizes what it means that the Messiah is choosing him, he starts feeling the weight. "Whoa, Jesus. Thank you for choosing me, but I gotta tell you, man, I'm just a fish-

NOTHING YOU HAVE DONE OR EXPERIENCED IS WASTED. GOD WILL USE YOUR HISTORY TO CHANGE SOMEONE ELSE'S DESTINY.

erman. I don't know how to do anything other than catch fish. That's all I know how to do."

Jesus says, "Let me tell you something. You don't have to learn how to do anything else. You're going to use the same skill set. You're going to use everything in your past. We're just going to flip it. Instead of catching fish, you're going to catch people."

Nothing you have done or experienced is wasted. God will use your history to change someone else's destiny. Get past your past. There's no future in it, but God will use your past for the future. That's what he wants to do with you today.

Live as a new creation.

When Jesus First, Jesus Always becomes your heart revelation, you experience a soul revolution, and everything changes. Jesus First, Jesus Always means it's gonna be different than before. He is the point. He's always with you. You are always with him. *It is finished* means *we* are never finished. He loves you; receive it.

Jesus precedes us.

Jesus overshadows us.

Jesus outlasts us.

Jesus first in pre-existence.

Jesus first in priority.

Jesus always in everything.

Jesus always in eternity.

Jesus first. Jesus always, and everything in between.

What are you gonna say when someone walks out on you, and you've been the faithful one? Jesus First, Jesus Always. What are you gonna say when you get the call you've been dreading, and the tests didn't come back the way you had hoped? Jesus First, Jesus Always. What are you gonna say when your dream is shattered into a billion pieces, and you can barely get out of bed? Jesus First, Jesus Always. What about when you're on a mountaintop, and your heart is about to burst with joy? *Jesus First, Jesus Always*. And when everything worked according to plan, and you're tempted to take all the credit? *Jesus First, Jesus Always*.

This is who you are.

This is the life you were meant to live.

NEVER
LOOK
BACK.

EPILOGUE:
what now?

If you have never invited Jesus—the real flesh and blood
Jesus—to become the Lord of your life, I want to give you
an opportunity to do so. As we have concluded, he has
finished an epic journey of love to reach you where you
are. He loved you on your worst day. Now you have the
chance to ask him to be a part of everything you are, and
everything you ever *will* be.

Pray this prayer out loud, with a sincere heart:

*Jesus, I invite you to become the Lord of my life. I recognize that on
the cross you gave your life for me and took my sins upon yourself
because of your great love for me. I am confident you have forgiven
me for the life I have lived without you. I will never be the same
after today. From this day forward, my life will be Jesus First,*

Jesus Always.

Amen.

When your purpose in life is to look like Jesus, to sound like Jesus, and to live like Jesus, it is obviously important to understand who Jesus actually is. Get yourself a great Bible. I love *The Message Bible* by Eugene Peterson. It is very readable and relatable in modern language.

It is also important to surround yourself with people who understand the hope of Jesus. Connect with a Bible-based local church that puts a premium on loving God and people.

Never look back.

ENDNOTES

1. Whiting, Bartlett Jere. E*arly American Proverbs and Proverbial Phrases*. Cambridge, MA: Belknap of Harvard UP, 1980. Print.

2. Berlin, Irving, Andrea Marcovicci, and Glenn Mehrbach. *Always*, Irving Berlin. Cabaret, 1994. CD.

3. Admin. "Top 25 Chuck Yeager Qutoes." CHUCKYEAGER.ORG. N.p., 17 Nov. 2016. Web. 07 June 2017.

4. Jobs, Steve. "IPhone Keynote Address." Macworld 2007. San Francisco. Youtube. Web. 7 June 2017.

5. Houston, Brian. *How to Maximise Your Life*. Castle Hill, NSW: Hillsong Music, 2013. Print.